Rules
of the
Road

Helps for Abundant Christian Living

By
Olivia M. Cloud

Rules of
the Road
Helps for Abundant Christian Living

Rules of the Road
Copyright © 1999 by The National Baptist Publishing Board
6717 Centennial Blvd.
Nashville, Tennessee 37209-1049

ISBN: 1-56742-050-8

Printed in the United States of America

Dedication

This book is dedicated to my mother,
Marjorie Banks Cloud, who helped me
learn, from a very early age, to
live according to the rules of the Christian race,
and to put them into practice every day.

Table

of

Contents

Introduction

The Christian journey doesn't just feel like a race, it is a race. From the moment we utter the words, "I believe," we embark upon a race. That race will be filled with godly adventure. There will be times when we think the race is over and we have lost. Suddenly, we regain the speed and momentum to be a serious contender in the race.

Just like stock car drivers in the Indy 500®, we must try to keep our eyes focused on our goal, which is our heavenly home. But just like any car race, many things can happen along the way. In order to finish the race, we must be well-trained, well-equipped, and well-prepared.

We also must be qualified to run the race by knowing the road rules. Our guidebook is God's holy Word, the Bible. We must continually refresh ourselves with the Book of wisdom and guidance He has given us.

Rules are only of benefit as long as we are willing to follow them. We must have both the willingness and the desire to be guided by the rules set forth by our Lord. *Rules for the Road* offers some helpful, biblically-based guidelines for running the Christian race. Each chapter contains Bible background information which serves as the foundation for our "road rules." By reading and doing God's Word, we are provided with examples for godly living.

Every driver on the speedway has a sponsor. This is the person who gives the driver the backing he needs to have all the proper equipment. Without top notch equipment, a racer cannot win. As Christians, we know who our Sponsor is. Through His shed blood, He has given us all that we need so that we can win the race. Our Lord has given us top notch equipment, as outlined in the sixth chapter of Ephesians, in order that we might be fully equipped to win the race.

Do you not know that in a race all the runners run, but only one gets the prize? Run in such a way as to get the prize (1 Corinthians 9:24, NIV) .

Every believer who runs the Christian race will receive a prize, yet we must run the race so that we can get the prize. A top-rate pit crew is necessary to win the race. The pit crew helps us to run well and to take corrective action when we find ourselves in trouble. Every Christian should be surrounded by strong believers who can offer ongoing support and who can help in difficult times.

You were running a good race. Who cut in on you and kept you from obeying the truth? (Galatians 5:7, NIV) .

On the roadway, we must pay attention and discern so that we can maneuver on the road. There are always obstacles and roadblocks. Christians must remain alert, always ready to meet the challenges we face as we pursue the prize.

CHECK YOURSELF

The section at the end of each chapter, entitled, "Check Yourself" is a guide for helping readers to put themselves in touch with these rules for the Christian race. Many of the questions are related to helping readers in personal development to help them determine their own points of strength and weakness in the race.

If this book is being studied in a group setting, the facilitator of the group should allow class members an opportunity to address questions of a more personal nature in silence. Provide each member with a pencil and paper for taking notes. Give them time to answer personal questions. Create discussion groups to dialogue about other questions. Use the questions of a more controversial nature to stimulate lively discussion within the group.

During the discussion time, differing opinions may arise. It is the responsibility of the group facilitator to manage the discussion process. One group member should not be allowed to dominate the conversation, including the facilitator! Members who are slow to participate should be asked questions directly in an effort to involve them into the discussion.

As you study these chapters, you have an opportunity to learn more about yourself as you race for the prize. Perhaps you will see glimpses of yourself in these Bible stories about men and women who forged ahead striving to do the will of God, pressing on toward the prize.

CHAPTER 1

Know the Rules

LET'S JUST DO IT OURSELVES

Now Sarai, Abram's wife, had borne him no children. But she had an Egyptian maidservant named Hagar; so she said to Abram, "The LORD has kept me from having children. Go, sleep with my maidservant; perhaps I can build a family through her." Abram agreed to what Sarai said. So after Abram had been living in Canaan ten years, Sarai his wife took her Egyptian maidservant Hagar and gave her to her husband to be his wife. He slept with Hagar, and she conceived. When she knew she was pregnant, she began to despise her mistress. Then Sarai said to Abram, "You are responsible for the wrong I am suffering. I put my servant in your arms, and now that she knows she is pregnant, she despises me. May the LORD judge between you and me." "Your servant is in your hands," Abram said. "Do with her whatever you think best." Then Sarai mistreated Hagar; so she fled from her (Genesis 16:1-6, NIV).

INTRODUCTION

One day, as I sat in a meeting about spiritual growth, one lady shared her morning ritual for starting the day with the proper focus.

"I have a letter wrapped in plastic that hangs in my shower," she explained. "I read it every morning just to remind myself who is in control." The letter read something like:

Dear Carmen:

Thank you so much for your interest. However, I do not need your assistance in running the world today.

Sincerely,

God

Of course, all those in attendance at the meeting burst into a sympathetic round of laughter. There are times when we all need to be reminded that we are not in control. Usually, it's at those times when we know the logical move for God to make. And as we wait, our logical human mind is ticking away, saying, "Okay God, this makes perfect sense to me. What are you waiting for?"

Some of you may be thinking that you could never become confused about Who is in control of this world. "Well, of course I know that God is in control," you might say. But do you really? Every sincere Christian will admit that he or she knows that the one true sovereign God rules the heavens and the earth. At least, that is the belief that most of us will confess with our mouths. But what about the testimony we give with our lives?

A few years ago, I had the pleasure of meeting a man who developed a study course which literally changed my life. Tim Sledge had grown up the son of a devoted mother and an alcoholic father. As an adult, he became a successful pastor, ministering to thousands of people. Over time, however, Tim began to have anxiety attacks. Through counseling, he learned to control the attacks. He later determined that he wanted to get to the root of the attacks.

Tim sought refuge at a codependency treatment facility. During a group discussion session, a fellow group member confronted Tim. "Who is your God?" he asked.

Indignant, Tim responded, "Jesus Christ is my God."

The man repeatedly asked the question, and Tim, now frustrated, gave the same response every time. After the session was over, someone came over to Tim and said, "Let me put it this way, who is in control of your life?"

It was then Tim realized that his relationship with God was not one in which he had given complete control to the Lord. Instead, Tim was trying to control everything around him, based on having grown up in an environment in which he was totally out of control.

IT HAPPENS TO THE BEST OF US

Abraham had about as good of a guarantee as a person could hope to get. God almighty personally had made a promise to him. A promise that was, as some have been known to say, "as good as a gov'ment check!" Abraham probably started out hopeful, having fully released his destiny to the hands of his God. He was a willing vessel — clay in the hands of the Master Potter.

Dutiful servant that he was, Abraham packed up his family and his belongings and started on a journey — a journey that had a question mark at the end. Every so often, he probably thought about God's promise to give him and Sarah a son. "I'm sure God will do it soon," he probably thought. And the years wore on with no heir. But Abraham and Sarah waited...and waited...and waited. After so many years passed, it just became down right ridiculous to think of two old people having a baby.

Surely Sarah never for a single moment consciously thought, "It's taking God a little too long to answer this prayer. Time to take matters into our own hands." Even though she never spoke the words, that's exactly what she said by her actions. She devised a plan to help bring about God's promise. Sarah indulged herself in a little creative thinking to make their circumstances almost as good as what God would do.

Hagar was of child-bearing age. And, since she was their servant, Sarah simply suggested that Abraham have sexual relations with Hagar and make an heir so that they could get on with this business of making a nation.

Whether Abraham was in agreement with Sarah, or whether years of marriage had taught him to simply "go along to get along," he did as she wished. He had sexual relations with Hagar and she conceived. Human nature being what it is, it wasn't long before the two women clashed. Sarah took out her frustrations on Hagar so she ran away. Hagar probably wanted her status elevated because, after all, she was carrying her master's heir. That, combined with the usual emotional upheavals caused by pregnancy, probably made Hagar a little difficult to deal with.

Sarah also vented her anger on her husband. She blamed him for what had happened! Meanwhile, Abraham was probably confused because he'd only done what Sarah said she had wanted. Now he was in the dog house. "Do whatever you want to with her," Abraham told his wife.

WHAT DO WE DO WITH ISHMAEL?

Abraham, Sarah and Hagar created a mess — one that only God could clean out and straighten up. If only they had obeyed God and been faithful to God's promises, this messy situation would not exist. What they created was a mess that could not be forgotten or swept under the rug. A life was created because of their desire to speed up

God's plan. Once Ishmael was born, what could they do with him?

A baby cannot be unborn. The results of what we create when we try to take control of God's domain can leave us baffled as to how the untidy situation can be handled — an illegitimate child...a soiled reputation...a prison term...a life destroyed...a spirit crushed...a family ruined. All of these are the kinds of circumstances that require God's redeeming love and mercy in order to mend. Once we have created disaster, divine intervention is required to realign our lives and the lives of those whom we have hurt.

The potential to inflict damage is what makes knowing the rules of the Christian race especially important. Too many people, church leaders and laity alike, have taken off from the starting line, carrying the torch and leading the pack in the Christian race. The problem is, they never bothered to ask the Lord if they were going in the right direction.

Those of us who profess Jesus Christ as Lord and Savior have a responsibility to know the rules, and to live the rules, each and every day of our lives. From the experience of Abraham, Sarah and Hagar, and perhaps our own experiences as well, we can learn much about the rules of running the Christian race. It is a race of endurance, requiring us to draw upon strength far beyond that which dwells within us naturally.

RULES TO LIVE BY DAILY

Rule #1 — God Is Always in Control.

Knowing who is in control and living our lives accordingly can save a lot of wear and tear on the mind, body, and spirit.

Rule #2 — Playing God Has Terrible Consequences.

Playing God is a dangerous game. One that has terrible consequences. If you doubt it, the Bible is full of stories about men and women who temporarily "lost it" and tried to take over God's job.

Rule #3 — If You Believe in God, Trust God.

The simple faith of the centurion is inspiring (Matthew 8:5-10). Even Jesus was impressed. Perhaps because the man understood the workings of power and authority, he willingly surrendered himself to the authority of the Son of God.

Rule #4 — Treat Others in the Same Way You Want Them to Treat You.

These words are a variation of what is often referred to as "The Golden Rule." Fortunately for his brothers, Joseph treated them like he wanted to be treated instead of retaliating with revenge (Genesis 45:4-8). Think of how terrible it would have been for Sarah if Hagar had an opportunity to treat her mistress as she had been treated!

Rule #5 — Never Give Up!

There are times when we give in, but we should never give up. Abraham, Sarah, and Hagar eventually came to their senses and sought the counsel of the Lord. Out of God's tremendous providence, God blessed them all. Abraham and Sarah got back on the path of being the forebears of a great nation.

Rule #6 — When You Stray from the Path of Righteousness, Get Back on it and Keep Going!

A provision that even we Christians do not always understand is that of God's grace and mercy. Grace abounds within our lives. God allows us to get back on track when we fall. There is nothing to be gained from years of brow-beating and guilt. Once we come to a point of repentance, the heavy load of guilt we carry has served it's purpose. Let it go! Move on and, the next time Satan tries to remind you of what you did before, do as Jesus did and say, "Get away from me!" Thankfully, Jesus has already paid the price of salvation. You don't have to crucify yourself to prove that you're sorry!

Rule #7 — Use Your Blessings to Help Others.

When God has been merciful enough to deliver us from our own sinful state, we need to help others by sharing the experience. There's an ex-addict, ex-thief, ex-liar, ex-gossip, ex-philanderer, ex-hypocrite or ex-"whatever" just waiting to hear your experience of hope. When you share the message that "God will do for you what God has done for me," you are spreading the Good News to someone is need of a powerful word from On High. God has not saved you simply so you can live in a state of self-satisfaction.

CHECK YOURSELF

1. Who is the Bible personality you identify with most?

2. Which of these "rules of the road" are you most likely not to observe?

3. Has there ever been a time in your life when playing has had a damaging effect on your life or someone else's life? If it has affected another, who is that person? Have you reached a point of spiritual growth where you can make amends to the person(s) you hurt?

4. Think of a time in your life when you either consciously or unconsciously chose to take over the reigns on control and handle a situation because it seemed to be taking God too long? What was the result?

5. Can you recall a time when you toughed it out and waited on the Lord to resolve a situation? What were the benefits you received as a result of your faithfulness?

6. Perhaps you have your own "rule" for Christian living that was not included in the seven rules given. Write it down on a separate sheet of paper. Commit to share it with others.

CHAPTER 2

Live Your Faith

When You're Sick and Tired of Being Sick and Tired

And a woman was there who had been subject to bleeding for twelve years. She had suffered a great deal under the care of many doctors and had spent all she had, yet instead of getting better she grew worse. When she heard about Jesus, she came up behind him in the crowd and touched his cloak, because she thought, "If I just touch his clothes, I will be healed." Immediately her bleeding stopped and she felt in her body that she was freed from her suffering (Mark 5:25-29, NIV).

INTRODUCTION

Robert Schuller, internationally known preacher and pastor of the Crystal Cathedral in Garden Grove, California, has said, "It is impossible to imagine something out of nothing without faith." An act of faith occurred as Jesus was on His way to Jarius' house. Through the rush of the crowd, Jesus felt someone living their faith.

Passages like this one show that Jesus is concerning about our every day needs, not just heaven (Mark 10:29-30). Many people were trying to get to the Savior - He was healing. The power that left His body informed Him that someone nearby had acted out of faith (Mark 5:30). Someone had dared to push through the crowd and find a way to get close to Him.

The unnamed woman, the subject of this illustration, was sick and tired, physically and probably emotionally, too. She had spent all she had looking for healing, yet to no avail. Her body had been losing blood for over a decade. By now, she was not only sick and tired, she was sick and tired of *being* sick and tired.

She was tired of feeling bad…tired of spending her money on doctors and medicine…tired of being an outcast from her community because her hemorrhage made her unclean (and therefore unfit to associate with). Likely thinking she had nothing to lose, the woman put it all on the line that day. She decided to live her faith.

Christians can talk faith, share faith, and explain faith, but all that is different from living our faith. It is not always easy to live our faith. Living our faith greatly defines who we are as Christians. Something in the way we live should set us apart. That something is our faith. If our living does not set us apart (sanctify) us, we have no witness for Christ. If we are feeling hopeless and defeated in the face of trials and tribulations, what witness have we to give to a hopeless and dying world?

The nameless woman gives us a powerful example of what to do when we're sick and tired of being sick and tired. She had reached a point where she had nothing to lose. Perhaps she'd even told herself, "If this is living, I don't want it any more." We do know from the text that she did have faith, however, enough faith to touch Jesus' clothes and be healed.

PERSEVERANCE

The woman was sick for twelve years. Yet, she must have never given up on the possibility of healing. She had to have seen the possibility for healing somewhere in her future. Surely there must have been many days and nights when she asked God, "How long?" (as did Moses, Hannah, Sarah and Abraham, David and others). She must have wrestled with every possibility, just as Jacob wrestled with the angel as he sought a blessing.

This woman exhausted all her resources trying to get healed. Doctors couldn't help her. Instead, she only grew worse. But she kept on. Because she refused to give up, she was healed as a result. One day I watched an interview with award-winning composer/producer Quincy Jones. He was sharing how he had been able to help a number of young recording artists get their start in the music industry. The interviewer asked him something like, "What's the biggest mistake you've ever made in judging an artist's talent?"

Jones replied, "I told Luther Vandross he would not make it as a solo artist." Of course, Vandross is an internationally acclaimed recording artist. Just think how different Vandross' life might have been if he had believed Jones! What if he had not persevered until he found someone who believed in his dream of becoming a recording star?

When we pray for healing — or for whatever we desire in order to achieve wholeness — it does not always come in an instant. Surely, the hemorrhaging woman began praying for healing the moment her sickness took hold of her. God hears all prayers from the moment they are uttered. The utterance of that prayer often signals the beginning of a faith journey which will lead us on to healing. It is the act of prayer that sets the faith journey in motion. It is also for that reason that people sometimes say, "Be careful what you pray for; you just might get it." That is why we must persevere.

We don't always know why it takes God so long to act, or why God sometimes doesn't act at all. The number twelve is a symbol of wholeness. Perhaps the twelve years of bleeding symbolized the completion of this woman's faith journey. Her time of healing came when she had persevered to the degree that she had no more money. Perhaps this was a lesson she needed to learn as part of her faith journey. On our faith journey, it's not enough just to get to the end, but to discover certain lessons along the way.

She came to Jesus, as she was, "weary, worn, and sad." Often we come to Jesus as tattered remnants. This woman is a symbol of the multitudes who have heard of Jesus, and who have available to them the resources of healing and wholeness, but who comes to Jesus as a last resort. It is amazing that many profess belief in Him, yet continue to turn to Him as a last resort. Sometimes we drag our suffering out by not coming to Jesus in the first place. Joseph Scriven described this phenomenon when he wrote, "What a Friend We Have in Jesus."

BELIEF

A good question to ponder is, would the woman have believed if she still had money to spend on physicians? Why did she cast her all upon Christ? Perhaps she had to be stripped of her financial resources in order to get down the bare essential — her faith. Desperation can increase our ability to believe in the power of Jesus to change our lives because we have nothing else to put our faith in, such as money, jobs or other people.

As she approached Jesus through the thick of the crowd, she likely felt she had nothing to lose. Her disease had made her an outcast in the community. She was unclean and probably had no husband or family. She probably carried an odor. No one wanted to associate with her. She was probably weak from twelve years of losing blood.

Her belief was simplistic, "If I just touch his clothes, I will be healed." After she identified herself to Him, Jesus told her "your faith" has made you well. He did not deny power had left Him, but affirmed it was her faith that made her well.

The woman believed with her heart, not her head. The head says, "After twelve years of bleeding, it's too late. Just learn to live with it." The head says there is no power in a person's clothing. She didn't have faith in Jesus' clothes, her faith was in the Man who worn them — so much so that she believed touching His clothes was all that was necessary. She confessed faith in Jesus' power. We also must confess the power and leave the manifestation to God. Consider the case of Shadrach, Meshach, Abednego or Daniel in the lion's den. That is what makes living in faith difficult. Living your faith means living in the knowledge of God's power and believing in that power, even if God doesn't do what we want.

ACT

Touching Jesus' garment was a bold act! This was an unclean woman — Jesus was a rabbi, a holy man. She could have been killed for such an act. Jewish law made her unclean, an outcast. Because she acted on her faith and did not allow herself to be caged in fear, she was healed and made whole.

Her disease had made her an outcast because of her unclean status. After she was healed, Jesus called her "daughter," which signaled that she had been brought back into the family. By uttering a single word, "daughter," Jesus told all who could hear that she was no longer outcast. Jesus brings us into the family when we confess belief in Him.

Her faith made her act boldly. Belief in Jesus Christ can and should make us bold, sometimes to the point of doing things that seem foolish. Human wisdom said the woman's act was foolish. It was foolish for an unclean woman to touch a man. But perhaps she felt twelve more years of bleeding wasn't worth living for anyway, so she took a faith step.

She acted on her faith, but she wanted to do so quietly and anonymously. Jesus would not allow her to remain hidden. He called her out. She was, so to speak, "busted." Perhaps He called her out because He wanted her to confess her faith. Perhaps He wanted her to eliminate her superstition and relate her healing to her faith, and not to His clothing. But by calling her to come forth, He was able to not only to heal her, but to bring her back into wholeness in the community.

The woman came forward in fear and trembling. We must remember that faith is not the absence of fear or unbelief — it is acting in spite of these things. The woman acted in spite of her fear. She had to act. She was only healed after she acted. Jesus was there all along, but if she hadn't touched Him, she never would have been healed.

Faith must have an object. Jesus was the Object of her faith and she reached out to Him. Jesus is the Object of the faith of every believer. Our faith does not have to be perfect. In the book of Hebrews, Abraham is called the "father of faith," even though he and Sarah tried to make a nation on their own because they grew weary of waiting on the Lord. But God fulfilled God's promise to them and gave them a son.

Hebrews also tells us that, "faith is the substance of things hoped for..." (Hebrews 11:1). This means living in the hope of what we cannot see. Living in the hope of what we cannot see is not easy. We have not seen Christ, yet He is our Hope. We must live in that hope from day to day and call upon our faith as a daily exercise in living.

CHECK YOURSELF

1. What are the three components of living your faith that are outlined in this chapter?

   _____   _____   _____

2. How does living your faith serve as a testimony to those who are seeking a better way of life?

3. Name two obstacles which could have easily hindered the woman from stepping out on faith?

4. Why do we so often wait until our backs are "up against the wall" before we become willing to turn our troubles over to Jesus?

5. Do you think the woman would have believed in Jesus even if she had not been healed after she touched Him? Why is it important that we Christians do not hinge our faith on the results God chooses?

6. Think of a time when you neglected to live you faith, based on the fact that you thought the problem was too petty to turn over to Jesus?

7. Why are seemingly afraid to come to Jesus with our brokenness, often waiting until there is nothing more we can possibly do as humans?

CHAPTER 3

Let Jesus Do His Thing!

He came to Simon Peter, who said to him, "Lord, are you going to wash my feet?" Jesus replied, "You do not realize now what I am doing, but later you will understand." "No," said Peter, "you shall never wash my feet." Jesus answered, "Unless I wash you, you have no part with me." "Then, Lord," Simon Peter replied, "not just my feet but my hands and my head as well!" Jesus answered, "A person who has had a bath needs only to wash his feet; his whole body is clean. And you are clean, though not every one of you" (John 13:6-10, NIV).

Passover in Jerusalem must have been an exciting time. Old friends and acquaintances getting together for, among other things, a lot of food and fellowship. For Jesus, it was a different time. He knew that His "time" was near, so He took off His clothes and wrapped a towel around Himself and proceeded to wash His disciples' feet.

When the time came for Him to wash Peter's feet, the disciple was opposed. He said, "No...never...!" Peter probably thought He was exercising great humility. Instead, the was denying himself an opportunity to get closer to the Master. He was denying Jesus the opportunity to "do His thing," that being to make us clean. The meal had progressed and the task had been undone. The Twelve were all too absorbed in their own interest to even consider giving service to someone else by doing a task as menial as washing feet. The One who faced death got up from the table in the middle of the meal to do the task Himself. Perhaps there was tension among the disciples. They may have suspected something was about to happen — but what?

Jesus wanted to bring them back together, to connect them by their bond, not divide them further with their selfish interests. The one thing they had in common was Jesus. He wanted to draw them in closer — to make them a part of Him.

IDENTITY

What does it mean to be a part of Jesus? Many people, Muslims, Buddists, Hindus, and even atheists, live highly moral lives. They live according to a code of beliefs or ethics that dictate their behavior in a positive way, yet have nothing to do with Jesus. For Christians, it is our discipleship that makes up a part of Him. Our obedience to Him connects and identifies us with Him.

You have probably known someone who professed to be a Christian, yet did everything except follow His ways and His teachings. If the person had not told you, you would never have identified him or her as a follower of Christ. Being a part of Jesus means striving to be like Him.

Many youth have been seen sporting the popular WWJD wear — bracelets, key chains, shirts, and so forth. It serves as a constant reminder that we should be following His ways. Many in our churches have been heard to say, "We must know who we are and whose we are." Christian discipleship does not evolve from a low sense of self, or in the words of "Amazing Grace" author John Newton, "a wretch like me." Rather, discipleship is rooted in our identity with the highest authority.

Jesus knew who He was. Jesus had been affirmed by His Father (Matthew 3:17). Likewise, when we have a strong sense of identity as Christians, we can be servants of Jesus and of one another. Instead, far too many of us often place the total emphasis of Christianity in one area. It is this distorted focus that makes it difficult for us to reach the masses who are confused and hurting, looking for a haven in which to rest their spirits. Jesus brought good news to the oppressed and downtrodden. He did not oppress them further by pointing out their inadequacies and making them feel inferior. He made them feel loved. For those who allowed Him to enter their hearts, Jesus did "His thing" and extended hope and salvation.

A common misunderstanding of our culture lies in our understanding of humility. It is a character trait that is not often lauded as desirable. Even in the church, many of us are reticent to put on the cloak of humility because it does not mesh with our self-image. Several years ago, when Andrew Young was mayor of Atlanta, he donned the disguise of a homeless man. He strategically placed himself in the parking lot of his church, a prominent Atlanta landmark, on Sunday morning. To his surprise, some of his closest associates shunned him. They did not see the city's mayor, a former United Nations ambassador. What they saw was a dirty, seemingly worthless man who didn't merit their time.

Others have embraced a false sense of humility, confusing a humble Christian spirit with low self-esteem. Jesus does not call us to be wimps and doormats, to be pushed around and bullied, all for the sake of a show of humility. "For God did not give us a spirit of timidity, but a spirit of power, of love and of self-discipline" (2 Timothy 1:7, NIV). God expects great things from us. We have not been empowered to let people step on us or abuse us. There is no glory to God when we allow ourselves to be used and abused. The kingdom of God is not served when we fail to take a stand and allow evil to go unchallenged because we believe we are powerless. Christians give a poor witness when we allow ourselves to be stepped upon based on a false sense of humility.

Contrary to popular belief, however, a humble spirit is not rooted in weakness, but in strength. One has to be strong and secure in his or her identity and self in order to be humble. Jesus left His place in heaven to come to earth and save us. He knew who He was and from whence He had come. He was Son...Lord...Healer...Counselor... Immanuel...Prince of Peace...Redeemer...King of Kings ...Lord of Lords...the Good Shepherd. Because Jesus was secure in His identity, He possessed humility that was beyond the capability of the disciples to comprehend. The Son of God was about to die a horrid death, yet the most important thing to Him at that moment was washing His disciples' feet.

Jesus didn't perform this menial task to create His identity as the Messiah, rather He washed their feet because of His identity. We also should give our service because of who we are, not so the world will know us, but so that they might know Him. Because we are His followers, we should always have a towel and wash basin ready for service! We cannot afford to think of ourselves as "too good" to do any task for the sake of the kingdom. Our Christian service cannot be done simply to establish ourselves as Christians. Instead, our service is rendered because we are Christians. Perhaps the reason many of us have so much trouble with humility is that we have connected ourselves with our worldly status and achievements more than with our status as disciples.

In order for us to rise to a level of humility, we must first let Jesus do His thing with us. He has to strengthen us and empower us so that we might know who we are.

When we know that we belong to Him, we can be obedient to Him.

LOVE

Jesus' foot-washing was not only an expression of humility, it was an expression of love. When we let Jesus do His thing, we allow Him to love us in a way greater than we have even known. Think about that Passover night. Maybe Judas knew, or maybe he thought they would simply imprison Him, not kill Him. In any case, he was about to betray his Teacher, and Jesus knew it. He also knew that Peter was about to deny even knowing Him. The others, He knew, would abandon Him out of fear for their own safety. Knowing all of these things, He washed their feet anyway. He loved them enough to serve them, even in the face of their betrayal. He knew them so well, yet He loved them in spite of their weaknesses.

Jesus knows each of us equally as well. In all of our fallacy and imperfection, Jesus loves us. Not just when we're good, faithful and obedient; He loves us even at our ugliest, when we are gripped by sin and shame. That love took Him to Calvary. Sometimes we make it hard for Jesus to do His thing with us in our lives because we cannot comprehend the depth of His love. Through His love, He can transform us from wretchedness to righteousness.

It seems ironic that one of the favorite hymns of the black church is "Amazing Grace." The song was penned by a man named John Newton. Once a notorious slave trader, Newton was known for his mistreatment and abuse of his African cargo. He had been known to beat, rape, and mercilessly abuse his human cargo. One day, as he stood on the ship's deck and looked out over the sea and the skies, there he became fully aware of God's greatness and his own smallness. He saw himself in his own wretchedness. The experience inspired him to write this famous song.

Although he is never described as a wretch, David was fully aware of his wretchedness. Yet, he was also deeply confident of God's love for him. In spite of all the things he had done, David knew with every fiber of his being that God loved him. The unlikely king learned to embrace what psychoanalyst later called the shadow self. Fully knowing his darker side, David praised the God who loved him in spite of himself.

When we are fully aware that we are loved by God, it creates in us humility that causes us to want to let others know and experience that same love. God's love does not make us selfish, it makes us want to share with others.

TRUST

Jesus trusted His Father. He wanted His disciples to know that same level of trust. The foot-washing was a lesson for them as well as an expression of Jesus' love.

As the disciples sat one by one, Jesus went around the room and washed their feet. The process was going along smoothly, that is, until the time came to wash Peter's feet. Never one to accept something he did not understand in silence, Peter was quite vocal with his objection. "No, Lord," he said. Peter would not let Jesus do His thing. He was blocking the way for Jesus to help him so that he could be a part of Jesus.

Have you ever said "No!" when the Lord tried to help you? When we say "No!," what we really are saying is, "I don't trust you, Lord. I don't trust that what you know is greater than what I know." By saying "No, Lord," Peter was not being humble. He was being disobedient. Trust in Jesus Christ cannot be separated from obedience to His will.

Another component of trust is vulnerability. When we allow ourselves to trust, we leave ourselves open — open to love, but also open to pain. When we trust children, spouses, co-workers, friends, we are vulnerable. They may not behave toward us the way we want or the way we think they should. But that's the risk we must take. The daughter for whom you scraped and sacrificed to send to college one day comes home and says, "I'm pregnant." The son we trusted to run the family business nearly bankrupts the business with because of his drug habit. The spouse we promised to love "until death do us part," comes home and says, "I'm leaving you." The company you devoted more time to than your family terminates you because of downsizing. The pastor you trusted and believed in is caught up in a public scandal.

When our trust is broken, we feel hurt and foolish. We feel we made a mistake for opening ourselves up to be mistreated by someone else. Some of us have even felt foolish for trusting God. Some people have said to themselves, "I was a fool to believe that 'wait on the Lord' stuff. I should have taken matters into my own hands. If I had, everything would have been fine." The experience causes many to build walls of protection to prevent such pain from ever gaining entrance into our hearts again.

Building walls around us does work. Walls are very effective barriers. It's entirely possible to build such a fortress of emotional and spiritual protection that nothing can penetrate. By building such walls around us, we can go though the rest of our lives without being vulnerable, and therefore without being hurt.

There's only one problem with building walls. They keep out hurt, pain and vulnerability, but they simultaneously keep out love, joy and peace. When we build walls, nothing can get in or out. In order to effectively block out the potential for someone to inflict pain, we must also block the potential to receive love. Once we build our blockade, our peace is also blocked because we must now expend our energy keeping the wall in tact. If someone threatens to enter our circle of trust, we must keep them out with the walls we have built. If the wall starts to wear down with time, we must reinforce the weak and worn spots by remembering those old hurts and keeping the pain alive so that the walls will remain strong and formidable.

The same principle applies concerning forgiveness. Jesus has said, "For if you forgive men when they sin against you, your heavenly Father will also forgive you. But if you do not forgive men their sins, your Father will not forgive your sins" (Matthew 6:14-15). God is always willing to forgive us for our sins. But when we are unwilling to forgive others. we have built up a wall of unforgiveness. That same wall we have built that does not allow us to forgive others, keeps us from being able to receive forgiveness from God. In being unforgiving, we thereby close ourselves off from forgiveness for our own misdeeds. To keep from building walls between ourselves and God, we must maintain divine trust, no matter what.

Jesus kept trusting His Father until the very end. Certainly, He did not want to die upon a cross. The human in Him wanted life (Matthew 26:39). Instead of giving in to humanity, Jesus yielded Himself to obedience. Because of His obedience to God, He has the power and authority to "do His thing" with us.

Jesus explained to Peter and the other disciples that a person who has bathed only needs a foot-washing. When we accept Jesus Christ as Lord and Savior, we have been bathed. Even though we have the assurance of salvation, we still need Him every day. We still need cleansing. As long as we live, there will remain a part of us that is unclean. During biblical times, a person could bathe frequently, but no matter how often the person bathed, his or her feet would get dirty because of the sand. With every journey one's feet would need to be washed.

Regardless of what we do on this earth — no matter how faithful, no matter how many good deeds, no matter how often we go to church or the number of ministries we participate in — there will always be a part of us that needs cleansing. Only Jesus can cleanse us completely. For this cleansing, we must submit ourselves to Him wholly and completely. It is through His touch that we are made whole. By allowing Him to touch us, we acknowledge our brokenness and embrace His healing touch. His is the touch of wholeness. He is thereby doing for us what we cannot do for ourselves. He is doing His thing. All we have to do is let Him.

Check Yourself

1. Has there ever been a time in your Christian journey when you have not allowed Jesus to "do His thing" in your life? In what way did you close yourself off from allowing Him to make you whole?

2. Have you ever built up a wall of protection because someone hurt you by violating the trust you placed in that person? If you have, pause and think about the situation and the person(s) that hurt you. Have you since allowed Jesus to come in and destroy that wall so that you can be made whole? If not, how has the wall affected your relationships with others and your ability to appreciate life to its fullest?

3. Why is it not possible to have trust without obedience?

4. Why was Peter's initial refusal to participate in the foot-washing ritual more an act of arrogance, rather than obedience and humility.

5. How does humility transform us and call us to obedience?

6. In what ways have you assumed a false sense of humility and denied the power of the Lord?

7. How does our identity as believers in Jesus Christ enable us to be humble?

8. Why is the Christian spirit of humility rooted in strength, not weakness?

CHAPTER 4

Recognize the Power of the Ordinary

In those days Caesar Augustus issued a decree that a census should be taken of the entire Roman world. (This was the first census that took place while Quirinius was governor of Syria.) And everyone went to his own town to register. So Joseph also went up from the town of Nazareth in Galilee to Judea, to Bethlehem the town of David, because he belonged to the house and line of David. He went there to register with Mary, who was pledged to be married to him and was expecting a child. While they were there, the time came for the baby to be born, and she gave birth to her firstborn, a son. She wrapped him in cloths and placed him in a manger, because there was no room for them in the inn (Luke 2:1-7, NIV).

The story of the birth of our Savior, as told in the second chapter of Luke, is a familiar one. If the story was about anyone other than the Messiah, it would be an ordinary tale. It is a tale of people who have to pay taxes, giving birth and fulfilling their obligations to the government. Joseph and Mary were ordinary people fulfilling the ordinary human obligations of their time. As has happened to many couples, the child of Joseph and Mary was not born under normal circumstances because they were not able to plan in advance. They did not have a lot of money, so they couldn't afford the best accommodations.

Sometimes, when we look for the movement of the hand of God, we are looking for it in ways and places that we would consider miraculous. Part of our Christian journey means recognizing that God does not need fireworks in order to achieve His plans. Surely many expected the Messiah to come like the Fourth of July. Instead only those who needed to know were told beforehand — Mary, Joseph, Elizabeth, and Zachariah. Imagine the circus-type event the birth of Christ would have been if everyone had known. At Christmas, we burn thousands of lights to celebrate His birth, yet God lit only one star to announce His arrival. People had looked for the coming of the Messiah for generations, yet when His birth happened most of the world knew nothing about it. Some of the greatest events of human history have happened in quiet, seemingly uneventful moments.

ORDINARY CIRCUMSTANCES

Many of the miracles of life happen in the day-to-day events. After the angel came to Mary and the others, their lives must have been quite normal. Mary and Joseph prepared for the arrival of their baby. Most likely, Mary had to deal with the every day complications of pregnancy that occur in most women. Joseph had to plan how he would take care of his new family. He was to become a father sooner than he had anticipated. The couple may have had to deal with the fact that people were counting months. Since their final step of marriage had not yet taken place when Gabriel spoke to Mary, people probably assumed that she and Joseph had engaged in their honeymoon a bit early. Amid the whispers of friends and neighbors, Mary had to hold her head up, knowing she and Joseph had done nothing wrong.

The fact that Mary and Joseph were so young must have been an asset. Often when we are young, in our naivete we are very trusting because we are too young to know that that's not the way it's supposed to be. An older man, nearing the age of retirement reflected on this phenomenon one day as we ate lunch together, "You know, as we get older, we worry more about security. When we are young, we say, 'The Lord will provide.'" The young couple must have put their trust in God. After all, Mary would be giving birth to the Messiah. Still, this did not exempt them from having to deal with the ordinary circumstances of life.

They were engaged in the ordinary circumstances of life as they made their way to Bethlehem ... as they engaged in their fruitless search for a room ... as they shifted to "Plan B" as Mary went into labor. But as they went from dwelling to dwelling, seeking shelter, they were shut out. They looked too ordinary. Nobody could have known this ordinary pregnant woman was about to give birth to the Messiah. Perhaps we shut Him out the same way, unknowingly, because the circumstances under which He comes to us are too ordinary.

The Christ child was born in an ordinary human way. Although technology has changed some, the way a woman gives birth to a child has not changed over thousands of years. In those days, a baby came when he or she got ready. It pretty much works the same way today. In the still, quiet night, another baby was born, just like so many others.

ORDINARY PEOPLE

Not only does God use ordinary circumstances, God uses ordinary people within those circumstances. Often we cheat the notion of the miraculous because we somehow deify the men and women of the Bible. We make them different from us. Somehow, we grant them more ability, authority, power, initiative, spirituality, and so forth. Whatever they had which enabled them to do God's will, we forget is present in our own lives, too. As we recall the story of how Moses delivered the Children of Israel from the clutches of Pharaoh, we remember only what Moses *became*. We tend to forget the man he was when God called Him. At the burning bush, Moses stood before God a stuttering fugitive, with low self-esteem. He could not see in himself what God saw in him. God saw beyond the man who stood before him because God knew what a great leader Moses would be some day.

Noah, Abraham, Isaac, Jacob, Deborah, David, Solomon, Ruth, Paul, Mary, Phoebe, Timothy and John were ordinary men and women, as was Harriet Tubman, Sojourner Truth, Frederick Douglass, George Washington Carver, Nannie Helen Burroughs, Martin Luther King, Jr., and many other human being who has been empowered to do great things for the Lord. God's empowerment makes ordinary people extraordinary. God takes us to a level higher than any to which we could raise ourselves. Therein lies the miracle. If we look for the hand of God in the lives of ordinary people we can see God's handiwork, molding and shaping them into usable change agents for the Kingdom.

Every person is ordinary and remains so except that God chooses and uses that person for service. God chooses every person for service. Once chosen, the question becomes, will that person God has chosen then chose to accept the call? Many of us remember a popular television show called, "Mission Impossible." Each week's episode was filled with drama, action, suspense and adventure. Each week, the IMF team was given a new assignment. Each week, Mr. Jim Phelps, the leader of the team, was given the option of accepting the mission or rejecting it.

Our life adventure with God is similar in many ways. God calls us into a divinely led adventure. We are given a mission. It will never prove to be an impossible mission, but it will be one that poses various challenges. No matter what the nature of the mission may be, we, like Mr. Phelps, have the right of refusal. God loves us enough to give us that choice. God wants us to freely give ourselves in service. Like the IMF team, our mission adventure with God will also be filled, at times, with drama, action and suspense. Jim Phelps and the IMF team always knew that, if caught, "the secretary will disavow any knowledge of your actions." Unlike the IMF team, Christians have the assurance of knowing, "Never will I leave you; never will I forsake you" (Hebrews 13:5, NIV). As long as we have been faithful to the call we have been given, our Lord will always be with us. God will, like the unknown messenger to Jim Phelps, go before us and make preparation for us to complete our mission.

Alone, an ordinary person cannot accomplish these things. With the help of the Almighty, however, an ordinary Christian can become mountain movers and shakers. The miracle in using ordinary people is that God uses us *in spite of* ourselves and our brokenness and *not because of* our own perceived greatness or ability.

EXTRAORDINARY MIRACLES

People expected the coming of Christ to be much different. When we pray for Christ to come and intervene, often we cannot recognize that His arrival because it is so ordinary. Generally, we expect Christ to enter with great fanfare, yet often the solution to our deliverance is already before us. We are often blind to the power of the divinely ordinary. Mary was a young single mother. She already had been told by the angel that she would give birth to the Messiah. But did she really know what that meant? As she watched her stomach grow, did she know that the baby inside her would one day cause the blind to see, the deaf to hear, the lame to walk and the sick to be healed? How could she have known all of the wonderful, miraculous acts her Son would cause to happen? As she sat in the barn and looked upon her beautiful new baby boy, she could never have known that He alone would offer salvation to an entire world?

It would be interesting to see what would happen if every young black mother took that attitude toward their sons and daughters? What if every child were looked upon as having the potential to do miraculous things. What if every mother and father looked at their newborn child and said, "My son/daughter will one day do great things?" Perhaps there would indeed be a lot more people doing a lot of miraculous things with their lives.

In our own lives, we can live expecting to yield the miraculous. Have you ever "just happened" to be in the right place to get a job that you need or wanted, to meet the man/woman of your dreams, to encounter someone who helped you complete a task you could not have done alone? Many people have had experiences of receiving an unexpected check which exactly covered the cost of a financial obligation. Others have been given reports of doom from doctors based on test results — upon later investigation, the condition had "miraculously" disappeared. Many of us can recall a time when something we feared greatly, something which kept us up all night worrying, never even happened because of human error, fluke or coincidence. Jesus can bring deliverance to us in the most ordinary ways.

When we look for Christ to come and deliver us, we have to set aside our expectations for a chorus of angels carrying harps, trumpets and drums. A preacher once said that, "the reason we don't like God's solution is that we don't like the way it's dressed. God's solutions often come in overalls and work boots." Some of us don't want to have to work our way through to deliverance. In the New Testament, Jesus came to those who needed Him. He still comes to those who need Him and He will continue to come. All we must do is wait on Him and do our part.

Very often, the miracle we seek lies in the very fact of its ordinary nature. Only through the power of an almighty God can greatness evolve out of such ordinaryness. The miracle occurs as ordinary circumstances combine with ordinary people to create an extraordinary result that is nothing short of miraculous.

CHECK YOURSELF

1. Think of someone you know who is rather ordinary, yet God used him/her to accomplish something no one would have ever dreamed? As best you can, trace how God moved in that person's life. Think of how that person was open to the call of God and the necessary remolding and shaping required to become fit for God's service.

2. Can you honestly say that you have kept yourself open and available to taking on a mission from God? If so, what is that mission, and how has God so empowered you? If not, what has kept you from making yourself available for service to the Lord?

3. Recall one instance in you life or the life of someone close to you wherein God intervened through ordinary people and circumstances. As the events unfolded, were you and the other parties involved aware of divine intervention in the matter? If so, what were the indicators of divine presence? If not, what blocked you and others from being able to seek the hand of God at work?

4. Name four prominent yet "ordinary" people in the Bible. What makes them so ordinary? How did God use them in spite of themselves?

5. How can you change your thinking and reorient yourself to expect God to yield miraculous results from ordinary people and circumstances?

CHAPTER 5

Discipleship Is Costly

For this very reason, make every effort to add to your faith goodness; and to goodness, knowledge; and to knowledge, self-control; and to self-control, perseverance; and to perseverance, godliness; and to godliness, brotherly kindness; and to brotherly kindness, love. For if you possess these qualities in increasing measure, they will keep you from being ineffective and unproductive in your knowledge of our Lord Jesus Christ (2 Peter 1:5-11).

Most of us know how it feels to be inundated with junk mail offering the promise of "free gifts." The irony of such solicitations is that, by it's very definition, a gift is supposed to be free. Our society is so full of gimmicks and schemes that people are suspicious of anything claiming to be a gift which imposes no obligation. Experience has shown most of us that there is a catch to the offer of that free gift.

Salvation is not a gimmick. It is free to all those who choose to accept Jesus Christ as their Lord and Savior. Yet, much like the "free gift" offers we receive in the mail, there is much more to the offer of salvation than

it appears initially. After our salvation, Peter offers a
direction for us to continue on the path to discipleship.
Salvation is free, but discipleship is costly. The call of
Christian discipleship requires that we do certain
things. The actions and attitudes we must take on,
according to Peter, are not those which come readily to
us. They must be cultivated in us, driven by our desire
to serve and imitate the One who has given us the gift
of salvation.

KNOWLEDGE

Knowledge of what a gift costs can cause us to appreciate it. The cost of discipleship includes knowledge —
not education, but knowledge, as in the saving knowledge
of Jesus Christ. The salvation He offers us is free. We cannot save ourselves or anyone else. It is a gift from God
that comes by way of Jesus Christ. It costs us nothing, but
it costs Jesus His life. The knowledge that we can do
nothing to save ourselves should bring forth humility and
gratitude. Our gratitude for having received eternal life
should motivate us to do all that we can to serve Him in
this life.

One Wednesday evening, as we sat in Bible study, the
leader asked, "What would you say to convince God that
you should be allowed into heaven?" As we went around
the room, many offered explanations such as, "I did my
best," or "I tried to be a good person." As the question
came to me and I thought it through, I realized that there

is nothing I can say to convince God of my eligibility to enter the Pearly Gates. My response was, "Lord, You should allow me to enter because You promised." Our assurance of salvation rests not with our own goodness, but with that of the One we serve.

Even though we cannot save ourselves, there is much that we can do to be better disciples. Doing things like singing in the choir, serving on the deacon or trustee board, working in the nursery, or serving on the usher board are not enough. Those are simply the housekeeping duties that come with being a Christian. Any homeowner knows that certain responsibilities come along with home ownership. There are certain things we must do. Likewise, there are certain things we must do as disciples of Jesus Christ.

In the passage given at the beginning of the chapter, Peter tells us the hard part of being a Christian. He lays out the cost of our discipleship: faith, goodness, knowledge, self-control, perseverance, godliness, brotherly kindness and love. These qualities do not come to us automatically, even when we are saved. We have to work toward them. They are the cost of discipleship.

EFFORT

On the occasion of my parents' twenty-fifth wedding anniversary, they received an assortment of gifts made from silver. It all shined so beautifully as it was displayed on our dining room table. After a few months, however, I noticed that the silver pieces which had been left exposed were beginning to lose their gleam. They were becoming dull and tarnished. That's when I learned about polishing silver. I discovered that it took extra effort for the silver pieces to retain their beauty. Likewise, it takes extra effort for the beauty of our salvation to remain in our hearts. And it will take more effort for some than others. But the effort we put forth as Christians should be contagious because of the inner peace and joy it gives us.

Peter's list of virtues may seem like climbing an uphill battle. But he gives us a realistic way to achieve this goal in that each one builds upon the others.

Faith — We must believe in Jesus Christ in order to receive our salvation. We must also believe in His power.

Goodness — We should give every effort to behave in a godly manner, treating others the way we ourselves wish to be treated.

Knowledge — Not only should we carry God's Word in our hands, we should carry it in our hearts.

Self-Control — Every Christian should make every effort to keep a measure of control over his/her actions, so that he/she is not swayed by every passing wind of change.

Steadfastness — The ability to "keep on keeping on" is a mark of faith and trust in God. In a distance run, as is the Christian race, the victory is given to the one who can hold out. We must know how to pace ourselves so that we are not worn our and unfit for the kingdom. The more we practice our faith, the more we are able to endure.

Godliness — a sense of personal piety is essential to discipleship. This is not to be confused with pomposity or self-righteousness. It is the difference between playing God and seeing God in all that we do.

Affection — brothers and sisters in Christ share a common bond. The Christian body is not a dysfunctional family. We are to regard one another with love and affection, the kind that is reserved for family. Being a part of the same family means we treat one another with the words of Paul from 1 Corinthians 13: we should not mistreat one another; we should not gossip nor be jealous of each other; we should not rejoice over another's misfortune.

Love (Agape) — the love we are admonished to have is not just for our blood family, or for our church family, nor for the body of believers that comprise our particular denomination, or for the family of our race. When we strive to be better Christians, we must love everyone, especially our enemies.

These seven "graces" given by Peter signify unity. Seven is a number which represents wholeness. Our journey to wholeness includes a number of virtues we are to strive to achieve.

DILIGENCE

Salvation comes the moment we receive Jesus into our hearts and claim Him as our Lord and Savior. But that is simply the beginning of the process. Discipleship is a journey of distance and endurance, helping us to build up our strength as we run the race. Contrary to the way things should appear, continuing on the Christian race makes us stronger; it doesn't tire us out. Peter gives us these things so that we will not fall on our Christian journey (1:4).

We are to add to the gift that we have been given, thus making it more valuable to us each step along the way. It is the continuous effort, the diligence, which keeps our faith alive. Unlike things made by human hands, the more we use our faith, the stronger and better it becomes. Our diligence makes us better Christians, improving our vertical relationship with God, and our horizontal relationships with each other.

If we do not remain diligent, we might forget what we could have become if not for God's grace. We might forget that we were headed for certain death and destruction, if it had not been for the Lord on our side.

As we diligently give and give and give of ourselves, we must never make the mistake of thinking that God owes us something back. God's gift to us has already been given. The gift we have been given can never be returned in its full worth. We will always owe God more.

Our diligence is required of us through times of triumph and trial. It is easy for us Christians to fall into a trap of believing that if we are good and do what is right, bad things will not happen to us. God did not promise that nothing bad would happen. Even though there is no guarantee against trials and tribulations, believers still can rejoice in the knowledge of Jesus' Words when He said, "I am with you always" (Matthew 28:20). Knowing that Jesus is with us all the way, we can be diligent in our efforts to run the Christian race with vigor and determination.

Bad things will happen to all of us. Knowing this, some people may think it's not worth the effort to strive to be better or do more for the kingdom. "If I try to do good and bad things still happen, what's the use?" they ask. The use is that our Lord has created in us a yearning. Though many people go through their entire lives and never recognize it as such, that yearning is for a deeper relationship with God. Some have strived to fill that yearning with pills, alcohol, money, sex, or other carnal thrills. There is no "high" like that which can be gained from an intimate relationship with the Almighty. When we face the difficulties of life, we can retreat to substances for consolation (which will never come) or we can see the solace of the One who loves us unconditionally, the One who can heal our hurts and discomforts.

Ours is a call to endure, to pass the torch and keep the message of the Good News going, no matter what twists and turns come into our lives. This is the cost of discipleship. Many are window shopping, admiring the goods from the outside looking in. Fewer persons have been willing to pay the price.

CHECK YOURSELF

1. Review the seven "graces" given by Peter. In what areas have you fallen short in terms of striving to be a more effective disciple?

2. Why are so many people window shopping when it comes to salvation because they are unwilling to pay the price of discipleship?

3. Like the tarnished silver mentioned previously in the chapter, what areas of your journey as a Christian have you allowed to dull and tarnish?

4. What would you say to the Lord in order to gain entrance into the kingdom of heaven?

5. Create your own chart for moving through the seven "graces." Determine where you are now in your journey. What barriers are keeping you from moving to a deeper level of discipleship?

6. What maintenance work have you done in the church because you are a Christian?

7. What work have you done to challenge yourself to grow further as a disciple of Jesus Christ?

CHAPTER 6

It'll Be Alright ... After While

When Martha heard that Jesus was coming, she went out to meet him, but Mary stayed at home. "Lord," Martha said to Jesus, "if you had been here, my brother would not have died. But I know that even now God will give you whatever you ask." Jesus said to her, "Your brother will rise again." Martha answered, "I know he will rise again in the resurrection at the last day." Jesus said to her, "I am the resurrection and the life. He who believes in me will live, even though he dies; and whoever lives and believes in me will never die. Do you believe this?" (John 11:20-26).

The saying "It'll be alright after while" is a saying familiar to most in the black community, most often among the company of elders. But the saying has great significance for us as we grow and mature in our relationship with Christ Jesus. My first true glimpse into this understanding came when a group from our church went to visit a group of senior adults at an assisted living high-rise. Though our group went to "cheer them up," we soon sat in silence, mesmerized by the testimonies of faith that came forth from among them. There were stories of people who had overcome predictions of terminal illness and other tragedies. Their stories were a testimony for any believer who holds steadfast that "It'll be alright … after while." They sat as living testimonies that our Lord does not turn a deaf ear on His followers. He hears every prayer and every cry. We simply have to grow into a trust relationship with Him. This relationship is very often the by-product of trial and tribulation.

The story of Mary, Martha and Lazarus is biblical testimony to this essential truth. Lazarus, the beloved brother of Mary and Martha, fell sick. The sisters sent word for their Friend, Jesus, to come and help; but He did not come right away. Meanwhile, Lazarus died and still Jesus did not come. After the brother has been buried in his tomb, here comes Jesus. He shows up after there is nothing left to be done. It is too late for the miracle they sought by calling Him in the first place … or so they thought.

When Jesus got there, Martha told Him, "Lord, if You had been here, my brother would not have died." How often have we thought a similar sentiment? "Lord, if you had been here…." When we are caught up in turmoil, we are apt to forget the power, wisdom, and sovereignty of the One whom we serve. We sometimes doubt that the situation will, indeed, "be alright after while."

This awareness usually comes to us in direct correlation to the length and depth of our walk with the Lord. This is not related to chronological age, but to spiritual maturity. The story of these siblings can help us to understand what it means to reach the level of maturity which assures us that "It'll be alright ... after while." The longer we walk with the Lord, the longer our track record with Him, the greater our assurance and confidence that He takes care of all things.

OUR LORD HEARS

The first thing the sisters did upon realizing their brother's grave condition was to call on their trusted Friend, Jesus. Some of the circumstances we face in life can increase our awareness of our need to call on Jesus. Mary and Martha sent a message to Jesus telling Him that "the one whom you love" had taken ill. This family had already experienced Jesus' love. He had been a frequent guest in their home. They knew the meaning of the words, "What a Friend we have in Jesus."

There is no mention made of a spouse being connected with either of the siblings. All they had was each other. They had no spouses or children. They did not have a high social standing. It was Mary who had anointed Jesus with precious perfume. The very act has raised suspicion concerning how a single woman in those days could earn enough money for such an expensive indulgence. Perhaps she simply decided to use the money to lavish this expensive perfume on her Friend and Teacher. Nothing was too good for the man who had brought back her brother from the dead and more.

When they called on Jesus that day, they had done all they could to help their brother get better, but to no avail. But they knew they could send a message to their Friend. We have that same privilege today. Jesus is no less a Friend to us as He was to Mary, Martha and Lazarus. Every believer can enjoy the privilege of Jesus' love and friendship, and the knowledge that we can call on Him any time. When we are in trouble, no matter what the trouble, we can call Him. Life will invariably bring us circumstances which are far beyond our ability to resolve. Sickness, loss of employment, loss of a loved one, loss of hope, financial troubles, and threats to the stability of our homes and families are all problems too can seem to be impossible. That is when it is time to call on our Friend, Jesus.

As Mary and Martha turned to Jesus, He turned to His Father, who heard His plea. As they were rolling away the stone, Jesus was already thanking His Father for having heard Him (11:41). Jesus knew that He had been heard. We must remember that we are heard when we call out to our Lord in prayer. When our backs are up against the wall, we can call on Jesus and He will hear us.

OUR LORD KNOWS

Even though Mary and Martha sent word to Jesus that Lazarus was sick, Jesus already knew more about the situation than they did. So often we fail to recognize and rely on the fact that God knows more about our situation than we do. We have only some of the facts. God has all the facts.

When Jesus arrived on the scene, Martha began trying to explain the situation to Him (v. 21). He already knew that Larazus was dead and that He would bring Him back to life. Martha assumed that Jesus knew nothing about what was going on and, more importantly, that He had chosen to neglect their plea for help because He was too busy doing other things. Very often, as we wait for an answer, it feels as though our Lord has not heard the urgency of our plea or that He simply does not have time to deal with our problems. In our prayers we try to explain to Jesus the desperate nature of the situation, fully forgetting that He knows what has happened and what to do about it. In the case of Mary and Martha, Jesus knew the event would bring glory to His Father. He knew how to best handle the situation.

How often do we forget that the Lord knows us and our circumstances better than we ourselves? All we have to go on is our own feeble understanding. With our limited knowledge, we accuse the Lord of taking too long to come and address our need. Mary and Martha watched helplessly as their brother drew nearer and nearer to death. Jesus knew their pain and He cared. He knew everything would be alright ... after while.

A difficult task for every Christian is to live in what I call, "the ellipses of life." Ellipses are those three dots of punctuation which indicate that something more is to come, and that something between what already is and what is to come is missing. Our struggle lies in the ellipses of life, in the after while. We grieve toil and struggle while we wait. Because we are believers, we know that the Lord has heard us, yet we wonder why He waits.

As we look at the case of these three siblings, they must have waited in a state of desperation as the questions flooded through their minds. They probably questioned His seeming absence in much the same way that we do. They likely tried to figure out His motives and plan of action. Surely, they asked: "Where could He be? Didn't He get our message? What's taking Him so long?", and the ultimate question, "Doesn't He care what happens to us?"

Our journey of growth as Christians disciples challenges us to trust in our Savior, knowing that everything will be alright … after while … no matter when the after while comes. As Martha stood before the Master hurt and grieving, her faith in Him still gave her room to believe that He could still make a different, even though from the human perspective the situation was deemed hopeless. Because of their faith in Jesus, in spite of outward appearances, the after while came for Mary, Martha and Lazarus.

OUR LORD ANSWERS

After Lazarus died, the sisters must have resigned themselves to thinking, "This is the way it must be." Possibly they were so distraught over the loss of their beloved brother that they didn't give it much thought after that.

When Jesus arrived, Martha came to greet Him. Mary was probably too grief-stricken to come out of the house. Martha, ever dutiful, came to Jesus as He was there at their request. Perhaps Martha was the oldest of the two sisters. In the tenth chapter of Luke, it was she who went about the house taking care of the matters related to preparing the dinner. Mary, on the other hand, appears to have been less confined by the need for convention and propriety. She tossed caution to the wind as she boldly went to the home of Simon to anoint Jesus. Mary, a woman with no husband, dared to enter the house of another in order to serve her Master. How many times do we neglect to serve our Master because we are afraid we have no permission or authority to go into certain places? It was Mary who left the chores to her sister while she eagerly sought the knowledge that the Rabbi could teach her. Although the two sisters were different, each of them held great faith in Jesus.

He had heard their plea and came in response to their plea, albeit, not when they had expected. When we make our own pleas before the Lord, we must remember that

His time is not our time. Instead our attention must be given, in faith, to the fact that Jesus already knew and held the solution before He came to them, even though He took His time about getting to them physically. As they fretted and grieved, they had no way of knowing that Jesus had the situation already at hand. The waiting was so they might experience the glory of God.

If we live in faith and are willing to wait on Him, we are able to experience the glory of God. That experience is the reward of waiting. When Mary came out and questioned Jesus' delayed arrival, He asked her, "Did I not tell you that if you believed, you would see the glory of God?" Instead of seeing their brother cured of sickness, they were able to witness him being raised from the dead. When we give ourselves and our circumstances to the Lord in faith, we are able to witness the awesome power of God.

When the glory of God is manifested, it is a magnificent sight to behold. The after while is the testing ground of our faith. Part of our salvation experience includes developing enough spiritual maturity to "be strong and take heart and wait for the LORD" (Psalm 27:14, NIV). Generally, we cannot know what is taking place in the interim before the after while. We cannot comprehend nor predict the sequence of events, but we can rest assured that God hears, God knows and God answers.

CHECK YOURSELF

1. How does Satan use your intellect to diffuse the strength of your faith as you wait on the Lord?

2. Recall a time in your life when you experienced the words "He may not come when you want Him, but He's right on time."

3. List five activities you can engage in to maintain and strengthen your faith in the Lord as you wait for the fulfillment of your prayer in the after while?

4. Find "What a Friend We Have in Jesus," (#340) in the *New National Baptist Hymnal*. Read the words and determine how they fit into the lesson of Mary, Martha and Lazarus. How have these words applied to your own faith experience?

5. Think of two potential crises in your life, over which you worried and fretted, yet never came to pass. How did those experiences impact your faith and assurance that the Lord can fix all things?

6. How has your relationship with God been impacted by the times when the Lord did not answer your prayer in the manner that you had hoped? Were you able to respond like Shadrach, Meshach and Abednego (Daniel 3:18), that even if the Lord does not bring deliverance, you will continue to do God's will?

CHAPTER 7

It's Not Just "Their" Problem

When Jesus landed and saw a large crowd, he had com-
passion on them and healed their sick. As evening
approached, the disciples came to him and said, "This is
a remote place, and it's already getting late. Send the
crowds away, so they can go to the villages and buy them-
selves some food." Jesus replied, "They do not need to go
away. You give them something to eat."

"We have here only five loaves of bread and two fish,"
they answered. "Bring them here to me," he said
(Matthew 14:14-18, NIV).

The life offered through the Christian faith is a wonderful life. But being a Christian poses a huge challenge
for most of us. Our society has taught us to be self-cen-
tered, to only worry about ourselves and our own. The
problem is that our faith challenges us to care about those
beyond our circle of comfort. Jesus not only challenges us
to care about them, but to also do something about the
problems they face.

People in the Western world, Christians included, don't
want to take any responsibility for the world's problems.

As we read about starvation, war, natural disaster, far too many of us respond, "Well, it's not my problem." Jesus' lesson to the disciples the day He fed the 5,000-plus people was, "Yes, it is your problem." It's so convenient for us to make everything "their" problem, "their" being an anonymous group of unfortunates who have no impact on our lives, nor we on theirs. We are quick to say, "I've got problems of my own," or "That's a personal problem." We try to shift the responsibility of fulfilling needs back to the one in need. Yet, if the one in need could remedy the problem alone, there would be no need for our help. We isolate ourselves from the true meaning of discipleship.

Even though they travelled with Him night and day, the disciples attempted to distance themselves from the needs of the people. They tried to distance themselves as their Teacher drew Himself closer to those in need. It took them a while to "get it." It takes us a while to "get" this thing called discipleship. Jesus used this opportunity on the mountainside to teach the Twelve something about what it meant to be His follower. In fact, this was the first time since they began following Jesus that they encountered a problem that was put to them to solve. Surely in their eyes, they had no reason to think about doing anything for anyone. Jesus was the Messiah who could fix all things Himself. What did they need to do besides follow Him around?

The hour had grown late. Jesus and the Twelve had already had a long day. Jesus had been healing and teaching all day. In a moment of concern for those in the crowd, the disciples suggested that Jesus send the people away so they could get themselves something to eat. They were being thoughtful, but not disciples. They wanted to send the people away. The Twelve didn't want to have any personal dealings with the people's hunger. It was, after all, their problem. The disciples were not related to nor personally responsible for any of the people who where there that day.

Jesus cut them off from their selfish train of thought by telling them, "You get them something to eat." He shifted the problem of caring for the people back to the Twelve. Probably Peter if none of the others thought, "He must be insane! How are we going to feed all of those people?" They told Jesus it would take eight months' wages to feed all of those people. Jesus issued them a challenge and they countered with excuses. When Jesus challenges us, we are prone to making excuses. We want to make the problem someone else's not ours. Why?

THE NEED

Jesus forced the Twelve to see a need they did not think was their concern. Jesus made them own the people's need. The disciples thought they had done enough simply by suggesting that He send them away. Jesus required more than mere courtesy from His disciples; He required service.

Sometimes the need He presents us with what seems so great, so overwhelming, that we feel compelled to shift the responsibility on to someone else. At other times, our own self-centeredness and greed makes us afraid to share what we have to help meet someone else's need. Our fear inhibits us. Meanwhile, Satan draws an illusion for us that makes the problem seem even more overwhelming so that our fear paralyzes us and we can do nothing. One of the great miracles of life is what Jesus does through us, in spite of ourselves, under the authority of His Father. Jesus takes sinful, selfish people and molds and shapes them into something He can use to bring glory to His Father.

Our immediate response, however, is to come up with catchy slogans and solutions to human misery and suffering. Our solutions are quick, causing no sacrifice on our part:

- Crime? "Build more jails for the criminals."

- Welfare? "Put those lazy people to work."

- The homeless? "Tell them to take a bath and get a job."

- Drugs? "Just say no."

- Teenage sex? "True love waits."

- Teen pregnancy? "Give them condoms and birth control."

- Domestic violence? "Just leave him."

- Sexual abuse? "Black folks don't do that stuff."

- Five thousand-plus hungry people? "Send them away."

The need overwhelms us. It seems far too great for us to resolve, and it is. When we consider our personal resources alone, we cannot meet the need. Thinking in human terms, thirteen men could not possibly feed over 5,000 people. But faith does not operate according to our sight (Hebrews 11:1). The Twelve did not see a way to feed all of those people, so they wanted to send them away, literally, every man for himself and his family.

Their limited spiritual sight caused them to shift the problem away from them, while they kept the solution to the problem all to themselves. The Twelve knew that Jesus would take care of their needs, yet they did not fore-see Him taking care of the needs of others. Often we are selfish, wanting to keep Jesus all to ourselves. We desire to keep His love, His power, and His friendship our own little secret. Our responsibility as Christians is to not only ask what Jesus can do *for* us, but what He can do *with* us.

Jesus probably smiled within Himself as He put Philip to the test by asking, "Where shall we buy bread for these people to eat?" (John 6:5). Philip and the others probably thought to themselves, "Do you know what you're asking us to do?" Jesus issued them a challenge and they coun-tered with excuses.

Many Christians have received a call from the Lord, a call which causes the heart to flutter and the mind to respond, "Lord, do you know what you're asking me to do?" Moses gave excuses to the LORD at the burning bush. Many who were issued a challenge from Jesus shied away, unwilling to take a faith step and forge ahead.

Just like He tested the disciples that day, Jesus tests us by putting before us a challenge that appears overwhelming. The call lifts us out of our comfort zone and into the faith zone. That day on the side of the mountain, Jesus demonstrated for them what it meant to be a Christian.

ACTIVE FAITH

Faith is not simply a noun, it is a verb. Faith requires action. Through faith, we are to act out of our belief that it has already been done. Preparing to take an airplane trip is an earthly example of how active faith should operate. Once our airline reservation has been made, we proceed to make our travel plans. Although we have not yet seen the airplane that will take us to our destination, we arrange for accommodations in the city to which we will be traveling. We pack our suitcase, taking clothes that are appropriate for our journey. Finally, we go to the airport an hour or so before the plane arrives and wait for boarding information. We have exercised active faith that the plane will be at the designated place at the designated time.

Jesus exercised active faith as He planned to feed the crowd. His first step was to instruct the disciples to assemble the people in preparation for the food they were about to receive. He prepared the people to eat before the food had even arrived! Sometimes we get so caught up in what we don't have, that we cannot make adequate use of what we have already been given.

After the people were assembled, Jesus took what they did have and gave thanks for it. He thanked the Lord for what they were about to receive. He gave thanks for what was yet to come. Many parents have prayed their children into a productive life because they thanked God for what their children would become with God's help. Before He gave thanks, what Jesus had to work with was meager — five loaves and two fish. Yet, He thanked God that this paltry amount would be enough to feed over 5,000 people. After He prayed, they were given all they needed and more.

GOD'S ABUNDANCE

God is able! Jesus understood this because He was one with God. We can never underestimate the power of God. The disciples did not have enough money to feed the people on their own, but that did not absolve them from the responsibility of feeding the crowd. Instead of thanking God for what was already there, they focused on the lack. We often forget to thank God for what we already have been given. They offered what they had and God's abundance turned it into more.

Over the years there has been scholarly debate concerning exactly how the people got fed. Some argue that the abundance was created by God out of nothing. Certainly, we know our God is able to do this, for God created our world and all that we know out of nothing. Others argue that many in the crowd had food to eat, but no one was willing to share because they all thought themselves to be the only ones with food. This camp asserts that the generosity of the little boy in the crowd touched the hearts of others who then shared what they had. None of the Gospels tell us exactly how the crowd was fed. It is easy for us to become so focused on the "how" that we forget God's abundance. Sometimes our own problems cannot be resolved because we will not let go of the "how." Since everything belongs to God and we believe in God, why do we worry about the how?

Because of Jesus' intervention, over 5,000 people were fed when there was no food in sight. That's a miracle any way it's calculated! God's will was done and the people were fed. Jesus came to show us that God is able to meet the needs of the greatest human challenges.

In meeting the problems that confront us as disciples, Jesus gives us hope for abundant living, not just materially, but spiritually as well. He is our Good Shepherd, guiding us out of our state of roaming, lost with no direction. He sees our vulnerability to the wolves and thieves which threaten to destroy us. He leads us to know that with God, nothing is impossible. He defuses Satan's lies, which tell us, "You don't have enough to help anyone else, so just help yourself." The master of deception tells us that everything will be okay even if we don't try to do anything to help.

Satan gives us fear. Our Lord and Savior gives us power and might to stand against that which seems too great for us to accomplish. He calls to our remembrance that "with God all things are possible" (Matthew 19:26).

CHECK YOURSELF

1. Name one aspect of the human condition that you find too overwhelming to attempt to take on.

2. What challenges have you left undone because of fear?

3. Think of a time when Satan's lies deceived you into thinking you were unable to accomplish something?

4. Recall a time in your life when you exercised active faith. How did the experience increase your faith even more?

5. How do you feel about the way in which the 5,000 were feed? Do believe it was one of those "ordinary" developments discussed in chapter four? Or do you believe the food was created from nothing as God did in creating our world?

6. How does focusing on our lack rather than God's abundance cripple our ability to do that which seems impossible?

7. Why do you think so many people in our culture have such an aversion to extending themselves to help others?

8. Go through your Bible and find at least three instances in which God promises to provide for us. Along your Christian journey, have your actions indicated that you believe in those promises, or have your tended to live according to what you can or cannot see as a possibility?

CHAPTER 8

Listen to the Right Voices

"When my life was ebbing away, I remembered you, LORD, and my prayer rose to you, to your holy temple. "Those who cling to worthless idols forfeit the grace that could be theirs. But I, with a song of thanksgiving, will sacrifice to you. What I have vowed I will make good. Salvation comes from the LORD" (Jonah 2:7-9, NIV).

Ours is a sophisticated age where technology rules. This high-tech living causes us to hear many voices — radio "shock jocks," television talk show hosts, outrageous sitcoms that offer everything but comedy. We are inundated with noise. Yet, in spite of all that we hear, there are really only two voices to be hear — the voice of the almighty God, and the voice of the enemy, Satan.

Both voices may come in different forms, through any type of medium. The irony is, the voice of God may direct you to do that which seems least desirable, while the lure of Satan seems to call us to paradise. Many of us have muddled our lives because we have not listened to the right voice:

• "You can do it and no one will ever know."

- "You can't get pregnant the first time."

- "Yes, I'm on the Pill."

- "You've got to cheat to make it in this world."

- "You won't get hooked like those others did."

- "A man wasn't meant to be with only one woman."

- "You can tell me. It won't go any further."

- "Of course I love you."

- "Just do it."

Those voices come to us in various forms, even from our loved ones. The troubles that those voices bring are often full blown long before we realize we have been listening to the wrong voices.

Jonah listened to the wrong voice. He had been summoned by God to go to the city of Nineveh and preach against them. But Jonah would have no part of it. He listened to a voice that told him, "Have nothing to do with those people." Therefore, he headed in the other direction, distancing himself from both Nineveh and God.

WE DO NOT BELONG TO OURSELVES

Jonah thought he was free to do as he pleased. And actually, he was, as long as he was willing to deal with the consequences of disobeying God. Jonah was a racist who harbored anger and hatred in his heart for the Ninevites.

He didn't want their lives to be spared. He wanted God to bring destruction upon them. Certainly, he did not want the messenger who caused salvation to come to the city of Nineveh. Jonah considered himself a child of God, yet he was unwilling to do the will of God.

Those of us who call ourselves children of God, must be careful. When we say, "I am a child of God," what we are really saying is, "I don't belong to myself." A great number of us who have followed the path God intended for our lives are not leading the kinds of lives we would have planned for ourselves. Every person is free to choose or reject God. Once we choose, however, there is no turning back. We no longer belong to ourselves. The right voices tell us that we are to seek out that which serves others as well as ourselves. The wrong voices tell us to think only of ourselves.

Jonah thought only of his own desires. He didn't really think about all the people who would be destroyed. He had probably devoted at least some of his time to thinking of just how God would destroy the city he hated so much. He didn't want to give them any advance warning. He just wanted to let them continue on their present course of destruction.

We Can't Hide From God

Jonah must have had a very limited view of God's omnipresence. He behaved as though he believed he could actually run from God and not be found. When we have been disobedient to God, most of us long for a place to run and escape. Some of us try and escape into substance abuse such as alcoholism or drug addiction. Some escape into the world of an eating disorder of a compulsion to exercise. Others try to escape into a glamorous and exciting lifestyle. Still others turn to workaholism to escape the fact that they are avoiding God's will. We may trot from place to place, but wherever we go God is there.

David understood that God is ever-present. "Where can I go from your Spirit? Where can I flee from your presence? If I go up to the heavens, you are there; if I make my bed in the depths, you are there (Psalm 139:7-8, NIV). We can spend our lifetime running to pursue our own interests. But when the Final Day approaches, no one asks:

- How much power did you accumulate?

- How far did you go up the corporate ladder?

- How many men/women did you seduce?

- How much money do you have in your 401K?

- How many people sought your autograph?

Disobedience cannot fill the void we create when we separate ourselves from God because we refuse to do God's will. When we try to escape from God, we are being disobedient. When we run from God, the heart can find no peace and the soul can find no rest. Jonah could not even take a simple boat ride. His great escape only landed him in the belly of a fish.

Sometimes God has to isolate us in order to get our attention. Jonah probably gained a totally different perspective as he sat in the belly of that fish. He even may have begun to think, "Well, I should at least go back and warn those people." He may have bombarded the Lord with a string of promises like, "Lord, if I just have the chance, I would do things differently this time."

Once we get quite long enough to realize that we've been listening to the wrong voice, the right voice begins to sound awfully good. God's voice sounds so good to us that we sometimes feel we have to make promises to God out of gratitude. Promises like, "If I ever get out of this, I'm going to …." As agonizing as it may seem to do the thing that God has called us to do, just think of how dangerous it is to actively go against God's will.

GOD EQUIPS WHOM GOD CALLS

If we listen to the wrong voices, we will be full of fear and worry about doing God's will. The wrong voices, those of Satan & Company, fill our heads with negative, limited thinking. From those wrong voices, we get all of the "what if's." The negative scenarios are the wrong voices! Those are the voices that will get us into trouble.

The truth is that God will take care of us. When trouble comes and others wonder how we made it through, it is because we have listened to the right voices. When we obey the will of God, our Lord will never bring us to a place and leave us alone. It may seem that way sometimes because we have listened to the wrong voices.

We are all prone, at times, to pay attention to the wrong voices. The voices that the Hebrews heard told them that they had left Egypt to die in the wilderness. Job, Hannah, Abraham, Rebekah, Elizabeth, Zachariah, and a host of others found themselves, at one time or another, listening to the voices of lack and limitation. When God calls us to a task, God equips us with everything we need to complete that task.

What does the right voice say to us?

"I will not leave you alone."

"The Lord will supply all your needs."

"You who are heavy-laden, come to Me and rest."

When we run from God's call, we should realize that we are running from our own inadequacy, never from God's ability to mold us. God sees all possibilities. A call from God is a high honor and a privilege. It signals to us that God is confident that we are able to accomplish a special assignment for the good of the kingdom.

CHECK YOURSELF

1. How has God equipped you to perform that to which you were called?

2. What are some clear ways to distinguish the right voices from the wrong voices? What kinds of things will the right voices tell us? What things will the wrong voices tell us?

3. Why do you feel is it important for us to be still long enough to listen to the voice of God and of those whom God sends?

4. God gives us free will, therefore, we really can do as we please. What are some of the consequences of doing as we please, no matter what God has called us to do?

5. Do you think promises made to God while we are in a spiritual fish's belly are sincere? Have you ever kept such a promise made to God?

6. Have you ever been like Jonah, preferring to perish rather than reach out to help someone you dislike?

7. Have you ever allowed walls of prejudice to prevent you from fulfilling God's call? What person or group would cause you to flee in the other direction should God call on you to serve them? Why do you harbor such feelings toward this person(s)?

CHAPTER 9

Don't Let Anyone Steal Your Dream!

Joseph had a dream, and when he told it to his brothers, they hated him all the more. He said to them, "Listen to this dream I had: We were binding sheaves of grain out in the field when suddenly my sheaf rose and stood upright, while your sheaves gathered around mine and bowed down to it." His brothers said to him, "Do you intend to reign over us? Will you actually rule us?" And they hated him all the more because of his dream and what he had said.(Genesis 37:5-8, NIV)

At age seventeen, Joseph was both the child of favor and a child of misfortune. Jacob held a special place in his heart for the boy. Having been born to Jacob at a very old age, Joseph was special. His father made no effort to conceal that fact. He even made a special coat for Joseph, a coat made from many bright and beautiful colors. The coat set Joseph apart from his brothers.

To further complicate matters, Joseph had a dream. His youthful naivete could not allow him to discern his brothers' jealousy. The lad could not know that by sharing his dream with his brothers he would incur their wrath. He had yet to learn the harsh truth that we all must come to know: everyone isn't happy to know that we have a bright future ahead of us.

Consumed by their jealousy, the brothers had no way of knowing that their having to bow to Joseph would end up being their blessing. They were just angry. They were angry about Joseph's coat, angry about love and attention their father lavished upon the youngest son. Perhaps more than anything else, they were angry because Joseph dared to dream while they consigned themselves to a life of mediocrity. If fact, Joseph's dreams even may have caused them to confront their own low expectations from life. As they tended sheep, young Joseph had the nerve to talk about a dream!

They all tried to steal his dream. Even his father rebuked him for his dream. Still, he kept the matter in mind. Jacob knew the ways of all his sons. Like most parents, he knew their abilities and shortcomings. Jacob must have known that his youngest son had the potential to do all that he dreamed about. In that same way, Jacob later knew which of Joseph's sons, Ephraim and Manasseh, would be the greatest. So often in life, people see in us gifts and talents we fail to see in ourselves.

The nature of a dream is tricky. Psychoanalysts understand the importance of dreams. Dreams are often God's mode of communication. They are often the way God gives us a vision of greater things to come. God may give us dreams in our sleep or when we are awake. Our God-given dream may come in the form of us seeing ourselves doing something we had not thought of before.

God-given dreams are powerful. Sometimes they are even frightening. What God has planned for us is so much greater than what we can imagine that it is frightening. Once that dream has been implanted, we embark upon a spiritual journey to make that dream come true.

YOUR DREAM WILL TEST YOU

Why would God test us for something God has given us? The first few months after I graduated from seminary, I couldn't find a job related to my field. There were times when I wondered why related employment seemed to allude me. I asked the Lord, "Didn't you tell me to do this?" I couldn't understand why the dream God had given me had not yet come to the time of harvest.

Often we need to be tested so that our character will grow to match our dream. Joseph had to learn some things before he could rise to the position of second in command of all of Egypt. Imagine the kind of leader Joseph might have been if Joseph had managed to escape slavery or escape jail. Joseph got the dream at age seventeen, but he was about forty years old before that day came to pass.

Another reason we are tested is to remind us that God's dreams are bigger than our own. God's dreams lead us to the conviction that, "I need God in order to make this happen." A God-given dream can only happen by the hand of God and through God's grace.

A God-given dream is always bigger than we are. A dream or vision from God is never self-serving. Perhaps Joseph's interpretation of the dream was self-serving initially. But years of hardship gave him the heart to serve humanity rather than the desire to be served. When God gives us a vision, it will be to the benefit of many.

Don't be afraid to put your own dream to the test. Ask yourself, "If my desire comes to fruition? Will it benefit anyone besides me?" If the answer is no, your dream is probably not God-inspired.

AVOID THE HUMAN TRAPS

As we faithfully follow our dreams, we must guard against the human traps which threaten to steal our dreams like a thief in the night. Even when God has given us a dream, there is always the temptation to take shortcuts to the fulfillment of the dream. When Jesus was in the wilderness, Satan tempted Jesus with food and drink as He fasted. He tempted Jesus with power as He sat in isolation, knowing Himself to be the Son of God.

The temptation of power is a human trap which can take us far away from what God has envisioned for us. God-given dreams are never about self. A person who is only interested in power and control only to have the authority to rule over others is not pursuing a God-given dream. One who understands the true nature of power does not seek power for his own sake. Dr. Martin Luther King, Jr. was a reluctant leader of the Civil Rights movement. He did not volley for position or authority. Others saw in him the qualities of a dynamic leader and they sought him out as one who could lead them. King accepted the charge. While true leaders do not seek power for the sake of ruling over others, they do not run from it either.

Another human trap is the temptation of pleasure. Well-known psychiatrist and best-selling author M. Scott Peck has asserted that the root of all mental illness is the desire to avoid pain. As God molds and shapes us to be fit for our dream, we will experience the pain of growth and change. If we seek to avoid this pain, we will avoid the growth which is necessary for us to move into the arena God has chosen for us.

The feeling that "almost is good enough." Accepting second best is another human trap. God pushes us to what is better, even when we would be satisfied with what we have already achieved. Sometimes, God pushes us forward by giving us a restless spirit. At other times, we may need circumstances to push us beyond our current comfort zone. Being Potiphar's trusted servant may have been good enough for Joseph, but it was not good enough for God. Being a prison trustee may have been good enough for Joseph, but it was not good enough for God. The Lord has to push Joseph to places of greater service. Each time,

Joseph was moved a step ahead only after he had proven himself faithful to that which he had been given.

Other dream-stealing traps include: a victim's mentality, thinking that one has no power to affect change; a need for retaliation or revenge; denial; cynicism; and defensive living, the "this won't happen to me again!" syndrome. Joseph could have used a number of excuses or defense mechanisms to keep him from going on to greater arenas. His brothers sold him into slavery; Potiphar's wife lied on him because Joseph refused to dishonor his employer; when he got to prison, the man he helped forgot about him when they could have helped him. Despite his trials and setbacks, in every circumstance Joseph earned favor and it was fruitful. His faithfulness eventually earned him an audience with Pharaoh.

When life gets us down or when people disappoint us, it's easy for us to respond, "I'm never helping another person again." It would have been far too easy for Joseph to decide that he would never help or trust another person in life. Thus far, all it had gotten him was what seemed like defeat.

BLOOM WHERE YOU'RE PLANTED

If anyone had a right to a defeatist attitude, it was Joseph. His own flesh and blood sold him into slavery. That's a painful thing to live with. But he didn't let that steal his dream. He was put in jail for doing the right thing. In every situation Joseph faced, he bloomed where he was planted. Instead of bitterness, Joseph chose honor and service. This is why God gave the dream to Joseph and not his brothers. The essence of who we are does not change. God saw in young Joseph a person of honor and high standards. God saw a young man with the potential to become a great and powerful leader. When we give what we have over to God, the Lord will refine us. The most beautiful piece of pottery and the strongest steel beam have both gone through the fire.

While we are in the fire being refined, how we respond is up to us. Will we allow our dream to be stolen? If it is taken away from us, it is because we have allowed it to be stolen. Suppose you had one million dollars in cash and you placed it on your front lawn. How long do you think it would stay there before it was stolen? Our God-given dreams are precious and invaluable. Yet, if we place our dreams in places or among people where they are not safe, those dreams will soon be stolen.

A dream is not fantasy. It is a vision of a higher place. The dreams God gives us requires something from us, too. God will fulfill the promise we have been given, but will we fulfill our responsibility? No matter where we might be at any particular moment, God is urging us to go further and higher, putting us closer to the dream. We cannot mope and moan waiting for the day of fulfillment. Until that time comes, we must give our best to the place where we are. Only if we are willing to bloom where we're planted can we be fit to enter into a greater level of service.

CHECK YOURSELF

1. What are some of the dream-stealers that have kept you from the vision God has for you?

2. Why do you think Joseph's brothers retaliated against him instead of taking issue with their father for showing favoritism?

3. Name three common human traps given in this chapter.

4. How can we distinguish between a God-given dream and indulgence in fantasy?

5. If you are presently facing a less than desirable circumstance, how can the determination to "bloom where you're planted" serve to change your situation?

6. Would you refer to Joseph's family as what we would today call a "dysfunctional family?" State your reasoning.

7. Think of a lifelong dream you have held. Put that dream to the test. Can it endure the rigors of a God-given dream?

8. Could you wait as long as Joseph for the fulfillment of you dream? State your reasoning.

CHAPTER 10

Enjoy the Beauty of the Scenic Route

When Pharaoh let the people go, God did not lead them on the road through the Philistine country, though that was shorter. For God said, "If they face war, they might change their minds and return to Egypt." So God led the people around by the desert road toward the Red Sea. The Israelites went up out of Egypt armed for battle. Moses took the bones of Joseph with him because Joseph had made the sons of Israel swear an oath. He had said, "God will surely come to your aid, and then you must carry my bones up with you from this place." After leaving Succoth they camped at Etham on the edge of the desert. By day the LORD went ahead of them in a pillar of cloud to guide them on their way and by night in a pillar of fire to give them light, so that they could travel by day or night. Neither the pillar of cloud by day nor the pillar of fire by night left its place in front of the people. (Exodus 13:17-22, NIV)

While we are driving, we sometimes make the mistake of making the wrong turn, causing us to miss the shortcut and forcing us to take a longer route. Many have jokingly referred to this as "taking the scenic route." We take the scenic route when we can't go the way we planned and the journey takes longer, both in terms of time and distance.

Just like when we drive a car, life sometimes does not go the way we planned — a missed opportunity, death, misfortune, financial setback, divorce, termination — all of these things throw us off of our planned course, forcing us to take life's scenic route.

Israel's journey to Canaan should have taken them only about two weeks or so. Instead it took them forty years. The Lord led them on a spiritual scenic route. The shortest route to their goal was not the quickest route to victory. The most direct route to Canaan was through Philistine country. For Israel, the most direct route was not the fastest route to victory, as God counts victory.

A person who has had the opportunity to travel to unknown places has no fear of getting lost. In the physical realm, a frequent traveler learns to relax while finding his/her way through to the destination planned.

In the spiritual realm, it is often much more difficult to trust God when we enter an unknown place on our journey. By nature, human beings cling to that which is familiar. Few people in this world are really adventurous, especially when it comes to spiritual matters. Not many of us are eager to venture into the spiritual unknown. Generally, we do not like change. Yet, there are times in our lives when God leads us into unknown places. We have to recognize when we are moving into a new spiritual place. More important, we need to make ourselves willing vessels to travel a new route. The call of a Christian disciple is a call to willingness.

OFF TRACK DOESN'T MEAN LOST

Just because the circumstances of life don't go the way we planned doesn't mean they're not going the way God planned. Moses, Aaron and some of the other men had likely laid out a travel route for their journey. They probably had planned to move from Egypt straight through the Philistine country on to Canaan. After they started on their journey, however, things changed.

For their own sake, God took them along a different route. The Hebrews were God's chosen. The Lord knew their abilities and limitations. God knew they were not ready to go straight into the Promised Land. A further reading into the text reveals that they still weren't fully ready even forty years later. God caused Israel to take the scenic route to get to their destination.

GOD IMPOSES SOME HINDRANCES

We must cease giving credit to the Devil for the work of the Lord. Every hindrance we experience is not from Satan. When we are faced with a road block, we are quick to blame the Devil when, in fact, it may be the work of the Lord. Usually, it is Satan who tries to trick us into taking shortcuts to victory. Satan lures us into being lazy so that we shun the delay caused by traveling through the scenic route.

If God has you taking the scenic route, know in your heart that it is for a reason. Sometimes God has to show us some things which can only be revealed if we take the scenic route. What we see along the way is the beauty of the hand of God at work in our lives. Instead of groaning and complaining while others seem to be zipping along the super-highways of life, we trudge along on the slow and winding roads, up hills and mountains, through valleys and lowlands as God sees fit to direct us. But in the process, we are being readied for service. As we travel this circuitous route, we often grow frustrated and weary. It is then that many of us begin to question the wisdom of God.

Once we have reached our destination in the way that God intended, we can often see why certain things have been withheld from us. Many times, as we look back over our lives, we find ourselves grateful for being forced into the scenic route. When we are caught up in the moment, however, we are generally consumed with the fact that things are not going the way we planned. Then we cannot appreciate the experiences gained along the journey. Sometimes we just need to relax and enjoy the beauty of God's scenery.

While we are on the scenic route, we can get in touch with valuable places of beauty. By taking the longer route, we have an opportunity to marvel at the wonder of God's handiwork as we become molded and shaped by the spiritual scenery surrounding us. We must look for the blessings which come from taking the spiritual scenic route, not the blockages.

GOD KNOWS BEST

Parenting teaches us to look at our children and to act and plan according to their strengths and weaknesses. A parent knows, for example, which child to leave in charge of the house in his/her absence. The children of Israel were God's chosen. God knew they were not ready to face the threat of war. In verse 17, God reveals, "If they face war, they might change their minds and return to Egypt." While God was preparing for their lack of readiness, Israel was preparing for whatever was to come. The Israelites probably thought they were invincible, ready to take on any challenge ... but God knew better.

It takes a great deal of trust in the Lord to travel comfortably along the scenic route of life. Our egos sometime get in our way, causing us to think we are ready for things when we are not. The churning of our egos causes us to become frustrated and impatient. We think that time is running out. We fear that at some point it will be too late for the Lord to help us.

The Lord provided for Israel and protected them. Even though God sent them by the longest way, their every need was supplied. During the day, they were protected from the scorching hot sun by a pillar of cloud (v. 21). At night, the sky above them was lit by a pillar of fire, allowing them to travel both night and day. Throughout their journey, neither the pillar of cloud nor the pillar of fire left their place. The God of providence always makes a way for God's people to make it through.

CHECK YOURSELF

1. In what area of your life has God caused you to take the scenic route?

2. What kinds of things might God show us as we travel on the long and winding roads of life?

3. How should we react as we watch others who seem to zoom past us, reaching the goals that seem so unattainable to us?

4. How does taking the scenic route help us to be better prepared when we finally reach our destination?

5. Think about the fact that the fastest route to victory may not be the shortest route. Recall a circumstance in your life when you were led to a greater victory because you were led along the longest route.

6. Do you think people ever willingly submit to taking the scenic route? If so, what could motivate such a person to be content with the fact that their journey will take longer than they anticipated?

7. Are many Christians like the man at the pool of Bethesda, not making progress because they are making excuses for their stagnation instead of trodding along the scenic route God has planned. How can we know the difference?

CHAPTER 11

Call on Jesus When the Storms Arise

That day when evening came, he said to his disciples, "Let us go over to the other side." Leaving the crowd behind, they took him along, just as he was, in the boat. There were also other boats with him. A furious squall came up, and the waves broke over the boat, so that it was nearly swamped. Jesus was in the stern, sleeping on a cushion. The disciples woke him and said to him, "Teacher, don't you care if we drown?" He got up, rebuked the wind and said to the waves, "Quiet! Be still!" Then the wind died down and it was completely calm. He said to his disciples, "Why are you so afraid? Do you still have no faith?" They were terrified and asked each other, "Who is this? Even the wind and the waves obey him!" (Mark 4:35-41, NIV).

The calm which the disciples enjoyed before being his by an unexpected storm is rather typical of our experiences in life. Jesus had spent a busy day teaching the masses. So many people came that He had climbed into a boat to teach them from the lakeshore. The people were listening, soaking in every word. Then Jesus decided it was time to move to the other side of the lake. Did Jesus know the storm was coming and decided to use this as an opportunity to teach the Twelve yet another lesson?

That day, the disciples collectively experienced a storm in their lives. Likewise, we can either collectively or singly experience storms in our lives. The storm may begin as a mere disturbance before it arises into a full-blown storm. It generally hits us suddenly and unexpectedly. The squall came upon the disciples unexpectedly. They immediately woke Jesus up. Did He not care that they were about to drown? When the storms of life cause us to feel as though we are drowning, we too might cry out to our Savior, "Can't You see that I'm in trouble?"

HELP!

In the midst of our desperate pleas for help, we sometimes feel as though our Lord is just off in the distance somewhere, perhaps sleeping as we perish. The Twelve had heard all of Jesus' teachings, yet when the storm arose they panicked. In our journey of discipleship, we may hear a legion of sermons, attend a thousand Bible study classes teaching us of the power of God, we sing thousands of hymns and songs of praise. Yet, when the storms of life arise, we panic and may even accuse Jesus of not caring about us.

In the text, Jesus asks the Twelve why they are so afraid. Why did they have so little faith? In their defense, the disciples had not yet witnessed great demonstrations of His power. Although He had taught and taught them, they had forgotten all of this by the time the storm came upon them.

Although they followed Him everywhere, they believed He was a great Teacher, the Messiah, they appeared to be afraid that Jesus would allow their boat to sink in the storm. Even common sense should have told them that God would not send the prophesied Messiah to earth, only to die in a freak boating accident! How many times do we ourselves become paralyzed with fear because we have not even considered what is true to the nature and character of God? Often we have allowed worry to hold us like a vise grip. We become afraid to move, afraid even to pray, fearing what may happen.

CALM REASSURANCE

The Twelve going to Jesus about the storm is analogous to a young child going into her parents' bedroom, saying, "There's a monster in my closet." While the parents know that there is no monster, out of love and compassion for their child, one or both of them will go and inspect the closet so that the child can rest easy. There was no real danger to the disciples, yet out of love and compassion, Jesus got up to calm their fears. Jesus was not motivated to help them out of fear, but out of love. He knew that everything would be fine, but His friends were afraid and needed reassurance.

Oddly enough, it was a combination of both faith and faithlessness which led them to go and awaken Jesus in the first place. The Twelve knew they were powerless against the storm. Therefore, they went to their only Source of help. Their faith had not developed enough for them to understand they were in no real danger, but they did have enough faith in Jesus to go to Him for help. They could not have known that even in His sleep, Jesus had the situation well under control.

They felt the need to go to Him and tell Him to get up! Their sense of urgency was great. They must have thought they could die at any moment. Were they warning Him of their impending doom? Or were they pleading for help. Yet, Jesus lay inside sleeping. Think of what great spiritual maturity we would have gained if we were able to truly rest in His love as the storms of life rage all about us!

BATTLING THE STORM

As the storms of life hit us, we can be secure in the knowledge that Jesus is very present among us, although the storm rages all about us. The boat may rock, the waves may rumble. The water may even come crashing into the boat. We may lose our balance and we may suffer some damage to the boat as we rally against the strong winds and waves. Yet, our Lord remains with us, even when it appears He is unaware of our circumstances.

When we call on Him, He will bring us peace, just as He calmed the waves of the sea. Jesus can bring us peace simply as an act of His will. After He has worked His miracles in our lives, we, like the Twelve, are left to marvel at His work. It is then that we realize we don't truly know Him at all. No matter how many experiences we have with the Master, we have so much to learn about Him still. As they watched the instantaneous calm come over the water, they must have been awestruck. Imagine how the Twelve must have felt, asking themselves, "Who is this man, really?" Perhaps at that juncture in their relationship, they knew there was something special about Jesus. They simply had no idea that He had command over the winds and the water.

Unlike the Twelve who were caught up in the raging storm that day, we have the benefit of knowing all about His awesome power. We know He has the power to cast out demons, heal the sick, raise the dead, and come back after the third day. A Savior powerful enough to do these things can surely take care of anything in our lives. Any storm which rages upon us can be calmed.

Jesus wants us to know how much He loves us. Didn't the Twelve know how much He cares? His is a perfect love. First John 4:18 tells us of His perfect love, which casts out all fear. We have no need to fear anything because we have the assurance of His love. Out of love for us, He calms our fears, even when there is nothing to worry about. He looks upon us, wrapped in all of our fears, and His heart is moved with compassion. He calms the storms of our lives with the touch of His hand and we marvel as all the chaos which once surrounded us and threatened to overtake us is stilled at His command.

CHECK YOURSELF

1. Think of a difficult storm that threatened to overtake you. In what way were you aware of the presence of Jesus? Did you feel Him near or did you think He was somewhere far off, unconcerned?

2. Do you ever give Jesus cause to wonder why you are so afraid when the storms of life press against you, just as the Twelve were afraid in the boat that day?

3. Name four instances in which Jesus gave visible demonstration of His power to those around Him.

4. Why is it that we cannot provide assurance to ourselves when we become like a little child who thinks there is a monster in the closet? Why do we still need Jesus to get up and offer us reassurance?

5. What will happen to a Christian who no longer goes to the Lord for reassurance concerning the storms of life. Does His reassurance increase our faith each time we require it?

6. Do you think Jesus set up the situation to occur so that He would have another opportunity to teach the Twelve about His power and His relationship to His Father?

7. In what ways do we underestimate Jesus' power, just as the disciples must have done that day?

8. Do you think the disciples awakened Jesus to warn Him or to solicit His help?

CHAPTER 12

Keep Your Eyes on the Prize

Therefore, since we are surrounded by such a great cloud of witnesses, let us throw off everything that hinders and the sin that so easily entangles, and let us run with perseverance the race marked out for us. Let us fix our eyes on Jesus, the author and perfecter of our faith, who for the joy set before him endured the cross, scorning its shame, and sat down at the right hand of the throne of God (Hebrews 12:1-2, NIV).

The words, "eyes on the prize" are familiar both to the black community and to the Christian community. During the Civil Rights Movement, it was a reminder of why they endured such suffering and degradation.

But what is the Christian's prize? Is it the glorification of God here on earth? Is it eternal life? Is the prize different for each of us. Certainly, every believer desires the heavenly prize. But there are also earthly prizes or rewards for which we must strive. As we run the Christian race, keeping our eyes on the prize, we must know what is relevant to winning the race and receiving the prize.

Being in the race requires that we are in a perpetual state of movement, of growing and doing. On the other hand, it is human nature to resist change. In the church, some of us have favorite pews, favorite positions, even favorite parking spaces which we are unwilling to share. All of this is going on as the world is crying out for help. The help that we can give them is offering them the Good News about the Savior who loves us; the help that our Savior has commanded us is give love to the world.

Concerning ourselves with things like favorite pews only serve to distract us and divert our eyes from the prize. When we fail to keep our eyes on the prize our lives lose focus and meaning; we forget our purpose in life. We live to glorify God in whatever we do, even in our weakness. The apostle Paul was given a message from the Lord concerning his own frailties: "My grace is sufficient for you, for my power is made perfect in weakness" (2 Corinthians 12:9, NIV). Those who are named in the "hall of faith" in Hebrews 11 had their own faults and shortcomings, yet they managed to keep their eyes on the prize and do the work which glorified our Lord.

FAITHFULNESS

Successful people, in any arena of life, have one primary goal in mind. They keep themselves focused on their prize. They are driven by the notion of attaining their prize. Often people are confused about what brings success. It is not necessarily brought about by goodness, but it cannot be done without faithfulness to the cause, whatever the cause.

It is faithfulness, not simply goodness that determines success. One who is faithful to the task of achieving a prize will do certain things to insure their victory. In the race we have entered as believers, there have been many faithful men and women. They were not always good, but they were certainly faithful. The eleventh chapter of Hebrews details the experiences of those men and women. When we go back to the primary Bible story which tells about them, however, we find that their experiences were filled with both high and low moments.

HINDRANCES

One who is competing in any sort of race cannot afford to be blocked by hindrances. Efficiency is important to a sure victory. In the automobile, much has been made over the term aerodynamic. An automobile that has been aerodynamically designed will allow for little or no wind resistance, which inhibits a car's performance. The flashy cars which were once designed with the huge tail fins were an eye-catcher, but they did nothing to aid the car's performance.

In the Christian race, we should strive to be aerodynamic believers. We can slow ourselves down with flashy things in order to attract the attention of others, but these things are hindrances. The sure victory will be to the one

who gets through the course with few self-imposed obstacles. Sometimes those hindrances come in the form of our
friends and associates. Jesus tells us it is better to lose a
body part and enter the kingdom, than to retain the
offending part and be thrown into the fire of hell
(Matthew 18:8).

When we accept Jesus Christ as our Lord and Savior we
begin a new relationship. We are no longer the same. We
sing a new song because He has touched us. That means
that things around us must change. The things which once
held us down, and the people associated with them, must
be cast aside. As we run the Christian race, we should be
dropping dead weight continually. With our eyes correct-
ly focused on the prize, we strive to be more like Jesus.

Salvation is a daily, continuous process. We are never
fully "there" as long as we live. There will always be
more for us to do to improve ourselves, no matter how
many years we've been in church, or how many people
we've told about Jesus.

PERSEVERANCE

The "great cloud of witnesses" we are given in Hebrews
11 are those who can attest to the goodness and power of
God: Moses, Noah, Abraham and Sarah, Hannah and the
others persevered to keep up the pace, even when the road
was at its rockiest. These persons, in all of their imper-

fections are our models for keeping our eyes on the prize to reach our heavenly goal.

In the earthly realm, we have another cloud of witnesses to guide and inspire us and keep our eyes on the prize. All around us, both famous and obscure, are persons who help show us the way to overcoming the human obstacles we face so that we can move on to the prize we seek. Racism, sexism, governmental persecution, physical disabilities, poverty, illiteracy and a host of other conditions could be used as an excuse to divert our eyes from the prize. Men and women like Fannie Lou Hamer, Thurgood Marshall, Arthur Ashe, and Florence Griffith Joyner fought to overcome what stood in the way of them and their dream. They persevered and they are not alone. In every case, there was still more to be done. But they, like we, must know that we judge our successes by the seeds we sow, not the harvest we reap.

God does not allow faithfulness to go unheeded. The victory is not to the fastest. The Christian race belongs to long distance runners, not sprinters. Flash-in-the-pan Christians, often full of charisma, may come and stir up a lot of excitement, but they are soon gone. Meanwhile, those who persevere may stumble and fall. They may have to stop and rest for a while and at times others may have to "prop them up on every leaning side." But they continue to heed the call which tells them to "keep on keeping on."

FOCUS

He is the author and perfector of our faith. An author is the one with whom a story begins. A perfector is one who smooths out the rough spots. Jesus does all of this for us. He is the One with whom our story begins. He is also the One who smooths out all of our rough places.

As we continue on the Christian race, we must keep our eyes focused on Jesus. If we keep our eyes on Him, we will not be distracted from our God. Remember, as long as Peter kept His attention focused on Jesus, he stayed above water. When Peter turned his attention to the strength of the wind, he became afraid and began to sink (Matthew 14:29-30). Our focus and attention must remain fixed on Jesus. That means running the race with blinders on — all that matters is Jesus. Have you ever noticed a toddler who has gotten separated from his or her parent in a crowd. Upon hearing the parent's voice, the child will run to that sound. No one else around the child matters, only the sound of the parent's voice. On this, we can take a lesson from a toddler.

Just think how different our journey might be if we were to keep our attention focused on the voice of Jesus calling us to do His bidding. As we look to Jesus, He looks to His Father. Jesus looked to His Father as He endured the shame, ridicule and pain of the Cross. When our own journey gets rough, Jesus refreshes and renews us along the journey if we allow Him to.

As we walk along the journey, people may talk. Noah must have looked awfully foolish building a boat in preparation for a flood with no rain in sight! People must have whispered about Ruth's foolish fidelity, choosing to stay with an old woman instead of finding herself a husband. The apostle Paul must have endured the sneers and jeers of mistrust as people all round him reserved judgement about his conversion. Regardless of what people may say, when our eyes are fixed firmly on the prize, however, we are undeterred. In fact, we are made stronger with every step along the journey.

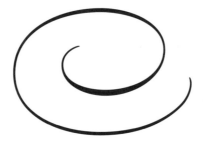

CHECK YOURSELF

1. What earthly prizes have you worked toward that required absolute focus and a sense of purpose? Were you able to attain that prize?

2. Think of at least two persons you know who have demonstrated their ability to keep their eyes focused on the prize of their heavenly reward. In what way did they manifest the gifts of blocking hindrances, perseverance, and focus? How has their journey inspired you?

3. What have been the major hindrances you have allowed to keep you from an earthly prize you seek?

4. Are you striving to be an "aerodynamic" Christian, casting off all things which inhibit your ability to run the race? If you still have things holding you back, what are they?

5. Why do hindrances become more difficult to eliminate the longer we hang on to them?

6. Why is faithfulness a greater determining factor of success than is goodness?

7. Why does our faithfulness take us farther along the Christian race than goodness?